RECONSTRUCTING THE PAST

Keith Branigan

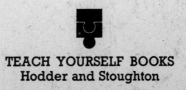

TEACH YOURSELF BOOKS
Hodder and Stoughton

First published by David & Charles 1974

Teach Yourself edition 1976
Copyright © 1976
Keith Branigan

ISBN 0 340 20388 9

Printed and bound in Great Britain for Teach Yourself Books,
Hodder and Stoughton, London, by
Fletcher & Son Ltd, Norwich

Contents

Preface

'Why are you digging it up?' 'How do you know how old it is?' In the short space of twelve years working on archaeological excavations I have so often heard these questions asked by onlookers. It is for the people who seldom get a satisfactory answer to such requests for information that this book is intended. It is written in general terms not for the 'informed' layman, but for laymen at large. I hope they will not be the only ones to benefit from it. Britain's professional archaeologists have decided that the 1970s must be the decade of 'Rescue'—the campaign to excavate and record as many threatened archaeological sites as humanly possible—and in this they are being splendidly backed by their part-time colleagues. Archaeologists in Europe and the United States are similarly aware of the hazards and opportunities facing them today. But 'Rescue', both as an organisation and as an objective, cannot be a continuing success story if it is carried on by archaeologists alone. It *must* win the understanding and approval of the public as a whole, as well as at least a measure of support from them. It is my hope that this book will play a small but effective part in achieving this.

K.B.

Acknowledgements

I would like to acknowledge the generous assistance of all those who have provided illustrative material for this book. My wife has read and re-read the typescript and made many helpful suggestions which I have gratefully incorporated into the finished text.

The author and publishers are grateful to the following for photographs included in the text:

G. Kelsey for Plates 2 and 21; D. Miles, courtesy of M5 Research Committee, for Plate 3; B. W. Cunliffe for Plates 4 and 32; P. Wade-Martins for Plates 5 and 29; P. J. Fowler for Plate 6; Minnesota Historical Society for Plate 7; Dr H. Kenyon for Plate 8; Winchester Excavation Committee for Plate 9; G. W. Dimbleby for Plates 10 and 11; B. Philip for Plate 13; Hester A. Davis for Plate 14; J. Hancock for Plates 17 and 19; the Ashmolean Museum for Plates 18 and 28; Museum of Archaeology and Ethnography, Cambridge for Plate 22; P. Ashbee for Plate 23; H. Catling for Plate 24; P. Warren for Plates 25 and 26; G. Reichel-Dolmatoff for Plate 27; D. Levi for Plate 31; R. S. Macneish for Plate 34.

1. Introduction to archaeology

Ever since the 1870s, when Heinrich Schliemann uncovered the remains of Troy and in doing so discovered a fabulous treasure of gold and silver objects, the achievements of archaeologists have been making headlines. Schliemann's equally sensational findings at Mycenae, where a rich array of weapons, jewellery and gold masks were unearthed in five shaft-graves, were followed not long after by the discoveries of Sir Arthur Evans at the Minoan palace of Knossos (plate 1). While Evans toiled in Crete, Hiram Bingham on the other side of the world scaled near-vertical cliffs in Peru to reach the lost city of Machu Picchu, almost certainly the Inca citadel of Vilcabamba. In 1922, before Evans had finished his work at Knossos, Howard Carter discovered the tomb of Tutankhamun. Beside the incredible wealth of precious objects in the four rooms of this Egyptian tomb, the discoveries at Troy, Mycenae and Knossos paled into insignificance. In 1930 Sir Leonard Woolley excavated the greatest of the royal tombs of Ur in Mesopotamia, and before World War II the remarkable ship burial at Sutton Hoo in Suffolk was found. The mid-1950s brought to light amazing finds at Jericho; the early 1960s the exotic mysteries of an 8,000-year-old city at Catal Huyuk in Turkey, and the later 1960s the palatial splendours of Zakro in Crete and Fishbourne in Sussex. The decade closed with the discovery of a 'new Pompeii' on the Aegean island of Thera.

In the public mind, archaeology is still very largely synonymous with the excavation of treasure-filled tombs and lost cities. The glitter of gold has made it difficult for the aims of the archaeologist to be seen in perspective. The layman thinks in terms of material objects and buildings, and judges archaeological expertise in terms of a knowledge of these things alone. But pots and pans, temples and tombs are not basically what the archaeologist is seeking; they are not the be all and end all, but simply a means to an end.

What then is archaeology all about?

According to Professor Grahame Clark 'archaeology may be simply defined as the systematic study of antiquities as a means of reconstructing the past'. Professor Christopher Hawkes gives a fuller definition: 'The purpose of archaeology is to discover, study and interpret the material remains which the prehistorians substitute for written history.' One would hesitate to quarrel with either interpretation, yet neither is entirely satisfactory. The archaeologist must concern himself not only with antiquities but the context in which they existed, and there are many archaeologists who are not prehistorians and have no dealings with prehistory. An eminent prehistorian may be excused for introducing prehistory into a definition of archaeology, but this book is concerned with the widest of archaeological horizons. Dr Glyn Daniel has rightly said that 'archaeology begins yesterday' and with the growth of industrial and post-medieval archaeology this is increasingly true. There is now a journal called *Post-Medieval Archaeology* which it is hoped will provide a timely reminder that archaeologists cannot ignore the early modern remains which so often appear in their trenches overlying those of the Roman or prehistoric period. Until recently, medieval remains also aroused less interest than those of earlier periods, and there is still less archaeological evidence for the medieval cities of Lincoln and Colchester than for their Roman predecessors. It is very often necessary for the archaeologist to excavate a series of levels and associated structures covering considerable periods of time and perhaps several totally different cultures in various stages of civilisation.

Whereas he cannot be expected to have an equally intense interest in each of these cultures, he should certainly excavate and record every level with equal care and skill. The fact that archaeology is the main source of information for the prehistorian should not obscure the fact that it can and does provide a great deal of knowledge about societies at various periods in history. Any definition of archaeology must take this into account and at the same time attempt to set out the responsibilities of the modern archaeologist. My own belief is that archaeology embraces the discovery, recording, preservation—where possible—and interpretation of all traces of man and the world in which he lived prior to the present day.

If this approximates to the modern concept of archaeology, then it is clearly a great advance from the days when excavations were undertaken principally to unearth ancient artifacts sufficiently sophisticated and complete to be regarded as *objets d'art*. Fortunately the pleasures of archaeology are not confined to such discoveries; if they were, then the majority of excavations undertaken in Europe and North America would not attract the thousands of volunteers who work on them each year. These volunteers come not only because they have a fundamental interest in the past but because they enjoy the task of archaeological detection. It might be said that detection is the aim of the archaeologist, and much of this book is concerned with the ways and means by which he detects and the problems facing him in doing so. It is in the field of detection, of course, that the archaeologist, who is intent on discovering all his clues *in situ*, differs from the plunderer. He will want to know the associations of everything he finds; discoveries made out of context will, unless recognised as such, completely falsify the evidence from which he will reconstruct his picture. Once artifacts are removed from their original context they are of little archaeological value, because it is the acquisition of knowledge rather than an accumulation of objects that is important.

For this reason, if no other, excavation has become a science in terms of the approach adopted and the techniques employed. It has often been compared to a laboratory experiment, but there is an essential difference, for excavation is by nature destructive and cannot be repeated.

Excavation, however, is only one-third of archaeology. There remain the study and interpretation of the evidence and, while the former is becoming increasingly scientific, the latter is still much less so. The archaeologist is trying to bring humanity out of a collection of artifacts, structures and scientific observations. He is therefore inevitably concerned with man's mind and intellect, even if indirectly by inference. If he is to succeed in reconstructing the life of ancient man in his surroundings, then he will need to employ the controlled use of his imagination. Only in this way can he hope to understand the mysteries of cave art or the problem of the Cycladic 'frying pans' (plate 2).

This duality of character in archaeology—of science and humanity—should not be seen as in any way a conflict of interests or a contradiction in terms. O. G. S. Crawford long ago put the situation in a nutshell: 'Archaeology is an art which employs a scientific technique.' As such it can provide one of the few genuine bridges between the 'two cultures'. In recent years there has been a trend in this direction. Certainly archaeological reports often include a whole series of specialist contributions by scientists of one discipline or another; a glance at recent volumes of the *Proceedings of the Prehistoric Society* will reveal articles devoted entirely to complex problems of bone identification, statistical sampling and similar topics.

The present age of 'scientific archaeology' is far removed from Sir Mortimer Wheeler's delightful pen sketch: 'The archaeologist wears corduroy shorts, strides about on draughty landscapes with a shovel and an odorous pipe, and is liable to be an undergraduate.' There are still a good many archaeologists who might be identified with this picturesque figure, but to some extent the shorts have been replaced by the white overall, the landscapes by the laboratory and the shovel by the microscope. The image has little to do with reality, however; the archaeologist himself rarely dons an overall or uses a microscope. Nevertheless, to the host of skills and attributes with which Grahame Clark, in his book *Archaeology and Society*, would endow the 'ideal archaeologist' must now be added a reasonable understanding of several sciences and the processes by which they can assist him.

Strangely, though the public seem to have accepted this new image of the 'scientific' archaeologist, the questions they put to the excavators when visiting the site of a dig are much the same as twenty years ago. Any practising archaeologist will be familiar with the eight questions on which the chapters of this book are based. My purpose is to provide the answers in such a way that the reader will not be confused nor the archaeological truths compromised. Most visitors to excavation sites do not care for the subtleties of strategy or tactics; they do not wish to know how carbon 14 dating works or what thermoluminescence means. Their questions are more direct and basic. While some relate specifically to a particular site and therefore cannot be answered in general terms, such questions as 'What have you found?' and 'How do you know what it was?' are posed so often that I have tried to answer them—the first by discussing the archaeologist's attitude to his finds and the second by describing how he builds up an interpretation of the structures and features uncovered.

The reader of this book should, by the time he has finished it, be better equipped to visit archaeological sites, to understand more of what he sees and to ask the sort of questions which will elicit informative replies.

2. Why are you digging it up?

This may not be the first question a visitor puts to an excavator, but it is one which commonly crops up as a conversation develops. It can be answered either by referring to the immediate circumstances which brought about the excavation or by discussing the much broader reasons why he and archaeologists elsewhere should be digging at all. Often an onlooker does not know what sort of answer he wants. One might seem satisfied with the information that, for example, the site is to be covered in for use as a car park; another clearly expects the archaeologist to justify not only his immediate excavation but all others as well.

Excavations can, at least in theory, be divided into three types. *Rescue excavations* are so called because their purpose is to salvage what information they can from a site shortly to be disturbed or even completely destroyed. In the industrialised and highly urbanised civilisations of the western hemisphere, transport systems alone result in the disturbance on a vast scale of existing land surfaces. The construction of motorways in Britain, for example, has presented archaeologists with a challenge extremely difficult to meet, necessitating dozens of rescue excavations (plate 3). In more concentrated areas, airport extensions have raised similar problems throughout Europe. Railways and canals, however, were in the main built before archaeological excavations had become commonplace. Though a mass of important evidence was lost thereby, it must be recognised that had these networks also been under construction today the pressure of rescue work would have prevented the recovery of much of the information whose loss is now mourned. By and large, it is the antiquities of the countryside which are most seriously affected by the disturbance and destruction wrought by present-day transport systems. Equally potent factors, however, are condemning the earliest towns to oblivion. A good many of western Europe's modern cities were once Roman towns which have been continuously occupied ever since. There has been endless building, repairing, demolition, rebuilding and destruction over many centuries. All such activities disturb or annihilate the buried remains of earlier towns. Today the pace of building and redevelopment is such that the archaeologist is under constant pressure to try and 'rescue' these now fragmentary remains by excavating them and recording—in advance of the bulldozers—the information they reveal. The creation of such new towns as Milton Keynes in Buckinghamshire once again carries the threat into the countryside.

The danger may be immediate and dramatic, as when the building of the huge Amistad Reservoir on the Rio Grande in the United States obliterated at least 400 archaeological sites; only two dozen were even partially excavated. One of the most destructive processes in western civilisation is often overlooked because its effects are felt more slowly and occur in a much less blatant manner. This is agriculture, which in Britain is probably responsible for wrecking more archaeological sites than any other factor. Stone Age and Bronze Age burial mounds, Iron Age field systems, Roman villas and medieval villages are all disappearing at an alarming rate as the result of deep ploughing.

Since ploughing is less immediately destructive than bulldozing, the excavation of sites threatened by agriculture is usually undertaken in spite of the threat not because of it. This leads to the second type of dig, *research excavation* (plate 4). This is normally carried out to find the answers to specific queries or problems. For example, Professor Atkinson undertook a series of excavations at Stonehenge in order to establish the sequence of construction. Where and how he dug were largely determined by the information he wished to acquire, not by the route of a motorway or the siting of a new supermarket. Archaeologists do not always want to excavate under the severe limitations imposed by 'rescue operations', despite their urgency; they realise that if such digs were the only source of archaeological knowledge, then these limitations would impose themselves on knowledge as a whole rather than on that of a particular site.

The third and least common type of excavation is undertaken to train new archaeologists (plate 6). *Training excavations* do not imply a lower standard of work, though they may progress at a slower rate. Many university archaeology departments run training excavations for their students, and there are in addition training schools, such as those at the Roman town of Wroxeter, which are open to members of the public.

These three types are presented here, for the sake of clarity, as separate and distinct operations, but in practice the divisions are often blurred. For example, a training excavation on the site of a Romano-British villa at Barnsley Park, Gloucestershire, is also a carefully controlled and planned research excavation. Where adequate notice is given of impending disturbance or demolition of a site, it is often possible for a research excavation, rather than a rescue dig, to be undertaken. In these circumstances, it may be reasonable to run a rescue, research and training operation in one. Thus, the immediate answer to 'Why are you digging it up?' may take one of several forms and reveal a multiplicity of reasons for the excavations.

There are deeper issues implicit in such questions as 'Why do archaeologists dig at all?', 'Why do they need to dig?' and, in the final analysis, 'Why archaeology?' Some of the more cynical members of the profession might claim that they dig only because they cannot earn a living in any other way, but most would admit that they do it because they enjoy it. There are times when digging is not entirely enjoyable—mid-winter in England and midday in Jerusalem spring to mind. But these moments are surprisingly rare and more than compensated for by those other times when discovery and detection lift the spirits and challenge the mind.

It would perhaps be more convenient and certainly more comfortable if archaeological detection could be carried out without actually having to dig the soil, but generally speaking this cannot be done. There are many aspects of man's past, even in historical periods, which either have no written record or are insufficiently or incompletely recorded. To appreciate this point, one has only to think of what has been learned about colonial forts in North America from the excavations at Louisbourg, or about everyday life in medieval England from excavated villages (fig 1). By far the greater part of man's existence has, however, been in a world totally without written records. For the

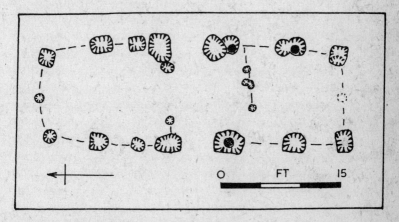

Fig 1: The plan of a three-roomed timber house (late eleventh early twelfth century) at North Elmham, Norfolk. Although some of the village history is known from written records, information about the form and construction of its Saxon and medieval houses has been recovered only by very extensive excavation. (*After P. Wade-Martins.*)

whole of this vast span of time, the only evidence for the development of man's religions, arts, technological skills, social customs, methods of warfare, and so on—in fact, for man's progress as a social and spiritual being—is that which survives in the form of artifacts, structures and deposits. In most places and for most periods in the past, these will have survived only if and because they are buried beneath the ground. In order to acquire the information they offer, there is no choice but to excavate them.

There remains the basic query: 'Why archaeology?' This has been often debated. Two fundamental values seem to me to justify its continuing existence. Firstly, there can be few other disciplines or fields of study which offer such a broad education. Archaeology is closely related to anthropology, ethnography and sociology. The student of the past must understand the philosophy and attitudes of the chemist, the physicist, the geologist and the zoologist, to mention only exponents of the more obvious sciences with which he has a working relationship. He need not know in detail how C14-dating is calculated or precisely how his metal artifacts will be examined and analysed, but he does require some knowledge of how the scientist thinks and what are his capabilities. Too much emphasis should not, however, be placed on this aspect of archaeology, for fear of under-estimating the importance of the humanities in the study of the past. In reconstructing an ancient society, the archaeologist is concerned with much the same facets of human behaviour as if he were studying a modern society—and think how many fields of specialisation there are for carrying out such a study today. For the past, there is no such proliferation of specialists, although there are, of course, ancient historians, philosophers, linguists and epigraphists. But these are concerned only with historical societies and, even then, there are few enough of them. It is fair comment that, in the field of prehistoric studies, there are archaeologists who specialise in the study of pottery, architecture, stone tools or metalwork. There is also specialisation in the broader aspects of ancient societies— the study of art, religion, funerary rites, subsistence economy and indeed the structure of society itself. When all this has been said, it remains true that those who specialise within these various fields are all archaeologists and that they will excavate, record, study and interpret a great deal of evidence far removed from their own particular interests. The archaeologist thus finds himself actively engaged in the study of the whole range of human activities, both physical and mental, from those as intangible as religious faiths to others as rational as technology. Any field of study which involves such diverse activities and demands such agility of mind may surely claim to offer its devotees a broad and valid education.

But what does archaeology hold out to the man or woman who does not participate in its pursuit and rarely if ever reads books about it? Such a question can be answered by another: 'Do we need history?' The end product of archaeology is history in the broadest sense of the word. Archaeology's contribution to it is, in essence, two-fold. In the first place it supplements the written sources and enables a much fuller account to be recorded. Almost all early documents were concerned with the great *events* of the past and gave little information about everyday life or the *processes* by which the manner, and sometimes even the nature, of daily living was changed. Archaeology, on the other hand, constantly provides evidence for processes. For this reason, it is archaeological evidence which contributes so much knowledge of the way ordinary men and women lived and worked in antiquity. Not only does it present a more comprehensive picture but a 'living' history, which can be more easily grasped and perhaps appears particularly relevant. The fact that so much emerges from the mute testimony of ancient pots and pans adds a new dimension to the story of man, enabling it to be seen, in a sense, 'in the round'.

Archaeology's second contribution to the study of the past from the point of view of the non-participant is that it greatly expands the period of man's known history. For the millennia before records began to be written, the only evidence of the story of man is that provided by the archaeologist. The importance of this evidence is not simply that more or remoter knowledge becomes available. By greatly extending the period of known history, archaeology has made apparent those broad trends and patterns in the story of man which would escape attention if only those centuries with a written record were studied. It has given history a new perspective and fostered a different approach to it; being concerned largely with processes, archaeology has encouraged people to look at history from this viewpoint, rather than as a series of events, however interrelated they may be.

But, whether it be derived from written or archaeological sources, is history needed at all? The knowledge, traditions and beliefs which make up today's society are the dynamic end products of history. They are held not merely because they existed, in developing forms, in the past, but because they were in some way recorded. Apart from historical and archaeological evidence, most records will have been in a form which cannot be understood or defined, but which might loosely and no doubt unsatisfactorily be termed 'human memory'. It would be foolish to suggest that if all historical and archaeological records were destroyed civilisation would collapse tomorrow or within the foreseeable future. As long as all those records were exempted which, by general consensus, would not normally be regarded as historical—scientific textbooks, research papers, etc—civilisation would continue to function efficiently. But its quality would be diminished and certainly a large part of the population would feel that they had been deprived of something valuable. This impression would increase rather than decline, as human memory gradually lost the 'records' of the past stored within it.

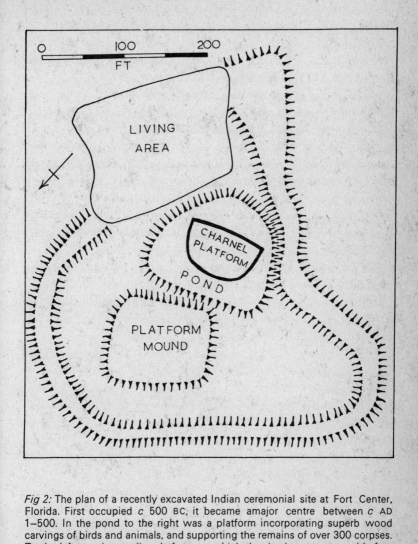

Fig 2: The plan of a recently excavated Indian ceremonial site at Fort Center, Florida. First occupied *c* 500 BC, it became a major centre between *c* AD 1–500. In the pond to the right was a platform incorporating superb wood carvings of birds and animals, and supporting the remains of over 300 corpses. To the left stood a smaller platform on which the dead were prepared before deposition on the main platform, while beyond both platforms was the contemporary living area. Much of the prehistory of North America has been recovered by archaeologists during the last twenty years. (*After W. H. Sears.*)

The feeling of loss would be a real one, for civilisation would have been cut off from something which is almost tangible—its roots.

If one doubts the value of history to a modern society, one has only to glance at some of those nations whose written story is relatively short. American archaeologists do not dig up pre-historic Indian settlements (fig 2) simply because they are there, nor have the Canadians excavated the colonial fort at Louis-bourg purely as an archaeological exercise. North American society needs roots, it needs a longer past, and the archaeolo-gists are providing them. The same is true of Australia and New Zealand, but this feeling is not confined to young nations. Who can doubt the value and importance of the excavations at Masada to the Jews, who have a long written history? Special stamps were issued and medals struck to commemorate the work. What is true of Masada and the Jews is true, in a less obvious way, of the Greeks and Mycenae and of the British and Stonehenge. Man needs a tangible past and archaeology holds the key to it.

3. How did it get buried?

The archaeologist, who spends his life studying the buried and excavated remains of man and his environment, is always a little surprised when asked this question. The answers, in relation to a particular site, or indeed to archaeological sites as a whole, would appear to be obvious. Yet paradoxically, in more specific circumstances, this is something that the archaeologist will need to ask himself. Often the way in which a layer or structure was buried will be a matter of considerable importance, bearing upon the history of the site being excavated. In whatever context the question is posed, however, the answer will fall into one of two categories. The first includes all the deliberate methods of burial, and the second those that are accidental or natural.

The most obvious reply to 'How did it get buried?' is 'Because someone buried it', yet this is true of only a relatively small number of archaeological discoveries. By far the most common example of deliberate burial is, of course, the interment of human remains, though in some climates and in some periods of the past human corpses have been exposed rather than buried. Burial does not always imply the digging of a grave, for not only have many peoples used caves as sepulchres, but others have built funerary chambers above ground or laid the corpse on the ground surface and then covered it with a mound of soil or a cairn of stones. Though deliberate burial of this sort normally involves a human corpse, it can and often has been used for other remains. Many human burials, particularly in the pre-Christian periods, were accompanied by grave-goods,

ranging from a single pot to thousands of them and a wealth
of other materials too. Some of the objects were surprisingly
large, like the chariots of the Marnian people who lived in the
East Riding of Yorkshire and in the Paris basin in the pre-
Roman Iron Age, or the furniture of the princes and nobles of
ancient Egypt. But these items do not always turn up as grave-
goods in a human burial. For example, the famous chariot from
Llyn Cerrig Bach, Anglesey, was buried in a bog as a ritual
offering. The solar boats of the Egyptian monarchs were
interred alongside the royal tombs, but not in them. Similarly,
though animals may be found in graves with human remains,
more often they were buried separately, and for different reasons—usually as diseased or useless carcasses, but sometimes as
sacrificial offerings.

Ritual burial provides numerous examples of articles deliberately buried. From the so-called Field of Offerings at Byblos in
Syria, for example, the French archaeologist Dunand recovered
many large pottery jars crammed with bronze weapons and
figurines and, less frequently, silver vessels. At the other end of
the scale are the few scraps of pottery and broken bone pins
found by British archaeologists in small pits dug within henge
monuments of the period c 2000–1500 BC. Sometimes it is difficult to identify with certainty a ritual burial of objects, and
there are undoubtedly a large number of ritual burials at present called *hoards*. The rich hoards of goldwork from the bogs
of Ireland, for example, were probably deposited for religious
reasons. Some hoards, however, owe their existence to a threat
to property. In times of danger or insecurity, ancient man
seems to have gathered together his most precious possessions
and buried them. For a variety of reasons these hoards were
never recovered and remain to be found by the archaeologist,
or more frequently by the ploughman or peat-cutter (plate 7).

The methods of deliberate burial so far described are the
more glamorous ones, where rich collections of artifacts and

the macabre fascination of skeletons often go hand-in-hand. Other methods are far more mundane, but to the archaeologist just as informative. For example, although ancient man made rubbish dumps, he also used refuse pits, and every time he dug such a pit he was consciously and deliberately burying material. Similarly, when his living-room floor became dirty and perhaps uneven, he would cover it with a new surface in order to bury the accumulated debris. But this comes closer to deliberate but unconscious burial and, in excavating the site of ancient buildings in particular, this factor has frequently to be taken into account. It was not simply a matter of ancient man demolishing one building to its foundations and erecting another over them. Often after demolition, the debris was levelled and used as a base for the new structure. In the Near East, where houses were built up to their eaves in mud-brick, the resulting depth of debris could be great.

Nothing can illustrate the process so clearly as the *tells*, or artificial hills, of the Near East. The *tell* of Jericho, for example, is a great mound more than 50 ft high, despite tremendous erosion, where once there was only a spring of fresh water. This man-made hill has resulted from six or seven millennia of construction and demolition of mud-brick buildings, together with the deposition of domestic rubbish (plate 8). But at Jericho, and other Near Eastern *tells*, natural as well as human factors have played their part in burying the past. Weathering eventually reduces mud-brick to its original state—soil—and Jericho, for example, is not a mound of recognisable mud-bricks but of the material from which they were once made.

Natural factors, which play an important role in burying the ancient landscape and the man-made features on it, are the ones which puzzle people most. To many people it is a mystery how anything as substantial as a masonry building can become buried beneath several feet of soil. Yet the early stages of the process can often be seen in the modern world. Once a building begins to fall into decay, its timber parts will soon rot, and even in a masonry building, this usually means that the roof will collapse before much time has elapsed.

Fallen, decayed woodwork and small particles of soil blown in through gaping doors and windows, begins to form a thin layer of soil on the floor. Here, and in cracks in the masonry or in disintegrating wooden window-frames and sills, small plants begin to take root (plate 5). There follows an almost endless cycle of decaying vegetation providing a rich bed in which more plant life grows. As the walls begin to crumble, more dust and small particles of soil are swept over the site by the wind. To this process other natural factors may be added. For example, if the site lies at the bottom of even a shallow slope, soil-creep and hill-wash will gradually bury the old surface, and the remains standing on it, beneath further deposits of soil.

This natural process of decay and burial can be, and often is, completely effective on its own. But in many cases it is assisted by human interference. This is particularly true of masonry buildings, whose ruins offer an easily accessible source of stone for further construction work. The removal of such material can rapidly reduce the amount of masonry to be buried, and may indeed result in the disappearance of the whole structure (plate 9). Timber buildings suffer less in this respect, though they decay more rapidly and produce richer humus deposits, so that they are soon buried. If stone and timber buildings can disappear within decades, then obviously less substantial features do so much more quickly. This is one of the problems being investigated today on Overton Down, Wiltshire, where archaeologists, who have constructed their own bank and ditch, are studying how quickly the ditch is filling up with scree and changing shape as its edges and walls collapse into the bottom. To compare it as it was soon after it was dug in 1960 and as it is today is at once to grasp the speed of the natural process of burial (plates 10, 11).

There are occasions when nature's haste seems positively indecent, as with the disasters which have buried archaeological sites, often very large ones, in a matter of hours. A well-known example is the tragedy of Pompeii and Herculaneum, buried by ash and lava as the result of the eruption of Vesuvius in AD 79 (plate 12). Recently, however, excavations on the island of Thera in the Aegean have begun to reveal a town, some 1,600 years older than Pompeii, buried beneath as much as 90 ft of ash and pumice, in a few hours of violent natural action. The centre of the island was blown to pieces by a gigantic explosion shortly after 1500 BC.

The richness of the finds at Pompeii, Herculaneum and Thera, and the remarkable preservation of the buildings is due, of course, not to their being prosperous towns at the time of their destruction, but to the nature of the disasters themselves. The towns were buried so quickly that the usual processes of decay were given no chance to operate, neither were the occupants allowed the opportunity to clear their houses of valuables and much of their property. Equally, the depth of the overlying deposits was a protection against stone robbing and the looting which often accompanies it.

The part played by natural disasters in determining the nature and the quantity of the evidence which survives has a parallel in the other burial factors. Deliberate burials of bodies, vehicles, hoards or rubbish may also be expected to yield a reasonable amount of finds. The very fact that someone has dug a hole with the intention of depositing *something* means that, all other factors being equal, one might reasonably expect something to be found in the hole if it is excavated. Furthermore, in the case of funerary burials, ritual burials and hoards, the artifacts are usually complete. But this is not so with accidental and natural burials. A building which has been abandoned and allowed to fall into ruin will often have been cleared by the occupants of anything valuable or even useful. While it still stands as a decaying shell, other people may make passing visits to it, removing anything which remains. By the time the building is finally buried beneath a mound of earth, its ruins will contain only broken fragments of pottery, food remains, useless containers and the like.

Other factors which determine the survival of ancient remains include the nature of the soil, the climate, whether the remains are organic or inorganic, and human interference with natural processes, such as mummification. These need not be gone into here. The point to be made is that the archaeologist not only asks himself 'How did it get buried?' and 'What does the method of burial imply in terms of the history of the site?', but also 'What has been the effect of the method of burial in determining the survival or destruction of the evidence?' Only when he has the answer to this will he be able to make a balanced assessment of the evidence which *has* survived.

4. How did you know it was there?

This question need never arise in the case of the many archae-ological sites which are permanently visible above the ground, such as the already mentioned *tells* of the Near East. These mounds stand out so clearly on the flat plains of Mesopotamia that their nature is apparent long before the visitor approaches close enough to see the mass of building and occupation debris littering the slopes and the ground below. The nearest parallels to these mounds in western Europe are probably the Iron Age hillforts, which utilised natural hills but festooned them with great banks and ditches to keep enemies at bay; these now serve as clear indications of an ancient settlement. But there are many other types of ancient site which remain plainly visible to the eye. Although Britain cannot boast any remains to match the Colosseum or the Acropolis, she has the walls of Silchester, the fortifications of Porchester Castle, and Hadrian's Wall. Further back in time, in the prehistoric period, Britain and western Europe produced few buildings and structures that were likely to survive the millennia. Among those that did are sacred sites like Stonehenge and Carnac, and thousands of megalithic tombs and barrow burials. Some of these, now called dolmens, stand on the landscape like primitive buildings, denuded of any covering mound they once had; others, still well covered by soil or stone mounds, are almost as easily spotted. But many thou-sands of barrows have disappeared completely (plate 19) and thousands more are now extremely difficult to discover. Just how *does* the archaeologist set about finding them and other archaeological sites which do not conveniently stick out from the landscape like sore thumbs?

If he is honest, the archaeologist will admit that very often he does not set about finding his sites at all; they are discovered for him. This happens in a variety of ways. Agriculture frequently brings new sites to light, as well as turning up innumerable stray finds and hoards. Many a Roman villa, for example, was first 'discovered' by the plough, while the digging of irrigation channels revealed, among others, the intriguing seventh millennium BC settlement of Nea Nikomedia in Macedonia (fig 3).

Quarrying, too, has been responsible for both the discovery and destruction of ancient sites. In Britain, areas so threatened are now the subject of intensive archaeological activity, such as that in the Welland Valley. Much of the gravel removed is used for construction work of one kind or another, and this frequently results in the uncovering of ancient remains. A great deal has been learnt about Roman and medieval London from excavations conducted as a result of the accidental exposure of archaeological remains by modern construction work. Only recently a major mid-first-century building was discovered in this way, and provisionally identified as London's first forum, or market-place (plate 13). The construction of roads and railways also brings to light remains of ancient rural settlements (plate 14). Nowhere has this been more vividly demonstrated than on the line of the M5 motorway in Gloucestershire and Somerset. As the initial earth-clearing progressed southwards, a string of hitherto unsuspected sites were revealed. These were mainly native settlements with no stone-and-mortar structures on them; consequently the sites have been in the past less easily detected than the contemporary Roman villas. The motorway has thus added a new element to the picture of this area c AD 50–400. Beneficial results have sprung from other unlikely sources. Dredging operations in California, for example, have

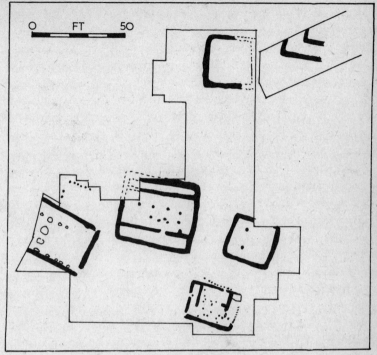

Fig 3: Plan of part of the Neolithic settlement at Nea Nikomedia in Macedonia. Dating to before 6000 BC, it was discovered during the digging of irrigation ditches and has proved to be one of the most intriguing early farming settlements in Europe. Among the site's many surprising features are the relatively advanced architecture of the houses, the double enclosure walls and ditch, and the large building identified as a communal shrine in the centre of the occupation area. (*After R. J. Rodden.*)

revealed many hitherto unknown early Indian sites which were covered by water. Marine archaeologists have been able to pinpoint and partially examine some of these. Even warfare has played its part in uncovering the past. Anyone who doubts the prospecting ability of the armed forces should consult Professor Grime's two fat volumes, *Excavations on Ministry of Defence Sites*.

Nature, too, takes a hand in archaeological discovery. Erosion in one form or another often exposes part of a site. It may be the work of the sea, as in the case where the breakers revealed a Viking cemetery in Deerness, Orkney, or the action of a river (plate 15). Violent and sudden exposure is rare but often more dramatic. Without the severe drought of 1853–4, the Swiss lake villages might never have been found and excavated, while the remarkable Stone Age village of Skara Brae, on the mainland of Orkney (plate 16), was initially revealed by one of those magnificent storms which strike the island's Atlantic coastline.

There is so much more that could be said about the ways in which archaeological sites are revealed by accident rather than design. My main concern in this chapter, however, must be to explain how the archaeologist prospects for his sites, for this is an important part of his work. Accidental exposures are largely unpredictable and beyond the control of the archaeologist. He must make what use of them he can when they occur. He cannot afford to wait for them to happen because when something is revealed by accident it is invariably exposed out of *context*. Every piece of archaeological evidence removed from its original associations, from the deposit in which it was originally situated, is evidence lost, not found. The archaeologist must therefore aim to discover sites *before* they are accidentally exposed.

But where to look, and where to begin? It would be foolish if the archaeologist in search of sites were just to launch himself into the landscape at random. The preliminary work in discovering new sites is done not in the field, but in the library, the archives and the map-room. The first step is to get acquainted with the geology and topography of a particular area, in other words to gain an understanding of the nature and shape of the landscape. Many archaeologists confine their search for new sites to areas where they have lived or worked for many years, because they have developed a 'feel' for them. Alternatively, a helpful start might be made by consulting maps and photographs, which will reveal a great deal about the shape of the

land and about the soils and rocks of which it is composed.
Maps will also show parish boundaries, footpaths, long-estab-
lished lanes and roads, which may all reflect older boundaries
or routeways. They will give place-names which often reveal the
location of ancient sites, such as the Roman *cester* (camp) or the
Arab *tel* (man-made mound). Others may be linguistically significant, like the Anglo-Saxon *ingas* names (Tring, Dorking) or
early Aegean place-names ending in *ssos* (Knossos) and *nth*
(Corinth). Such clues to boundaries, routes and ancient sites
can be gained from quite ordinary and easily obtainable maps.
More detailed and specific clues must usually be sought in older
and less widely distributed maps or in parish records, from
which the original field names of a chosen area can be gradually
accumulated. Some of these names may be suggestive of earlier
discoveries of building debris or foundations (Tile Field, Chapel
Field, Stoney Field), while others (Kiln Field, Oven Field) may
reflect the appearance of kiln or destruction debris. Such field
names can never be regarded as firm evidence for the existence
of ancient remains, but they provide clues which, together with
further research and fieldwork, may lead to their discovery.

Parish records also produce many references to stray finds
of antiquities and to ancient structures still visible two or three
centuries ago but now completely destroyed, at least above
ground level. The same is true of a good many books written in
the eighteenth and nineteenth centuries, and not only those
purporting to be about antiquities. From all these sources the
archaeologist may reasonably hope to discover clues to the
location of ancient sites. If he is fortunate he will, in addition, be
able to examine the accessions registers of his local museums,
where are recorded many more examples of stray finds which
eventually passed into their collections. He will also have
available the reports on previously discovered and excavated
sites in his area. This information should enable him to understand something of their nature, the sort of material they will

produce, the economy on which they were based and the sort
of locations in which they were placed. All these points will help
him to know where to look and what to look for.

The archaeologist may now be able to take his work a stage
farther before starting work in the field. It is rare, in either the
ancient or modern world, for settlement patterns not to have
rhyme and reason; indeed the term 'pattern' implies as much.
By plotting his information on to a map or a series of maps the
archaeologist may be able to see the pattern emerging and to
understand something of the rhyme and reason behind it. If he
can do this, he will be well on the way to finding his new sites.

All this desk work may seem far removed from walking over
muddy fields in search of telltale scraps of pottery and flint, but
it is a necessary precursor of this activity. Having exhausted the
information derived from books, records and maps, the archaeologist must now see how much he can wring from the landscape
itself. Today, many surveys intensively search several square
miles of land in order to fully establish the pattern of human
settlements from the earliest times to the present day. The results and the density of the finds are sometimes staggering. In
the Tehuacan valley, Mexico, an American team found over 450
sites, dating from about 10 000 BC to AD 1500. This particular
survey was tied to an extensive excavation programme, so that
subsequently twelve key sites were excavated.

In some parts of the world and particularly in western
Europe, survey work is greatly assisted by aerial photography.
This method reveals three principal types of site, two of which
would be almost impossible to identify from ground level.
Shadow sites, photographed from a low altitude and with the
sun at a low point in the sky, are recognisable on the ground as
a series of earthworks—low banks, ditches, mounds, depressions
and so on. From the air they take on form and a relationship to
one another (plate 17); sometimes such earthworks have been so
destroyed that they are only visible from the air in the condi-

tions mentioned. *Crop marks*, where crops or vegetation are growing at different rates and producing different colouring due to subterranean features of one sort or another, are almost impossible to see from the ground, at least as recognisable patterns. From the air they show very clearly indeed (plate 18). Similarly, *soil mark* sites are difficult to recognise and impossible to disentangle at ground level, but quickly form a pattern from the air (plate 19). Soil marks occur where ancient man has introduced anomalies into the topsoil. Material may have been dug from lower levels during the cutting of a ditch or pit, or introduced from elsewhere, such as clay to form a building platform, or even stone and mortar for use in buildings. It might be thought that aerial photography, since it can reveal sites so easily and in such a readily understandable way, obviates the need for field-walking, but this is not so. For one thing, aerial photography is not as simple as it seems. Crop marks, for example, only occur under certain geological and climatic conditions, and even then may only be visible for a few days or at best a week or two. Furthermore their interpretation needs considerable care; not all the features seen need be man-made. The colouring of the crops varies not only according to the type of subterranean feature over which they are growing, but also according to the type of crop itself and the stage of growth at the time it is photographed. Many early prehistoric communities may not have built earthworks large enough or dug ditches deep enough to produce shadows, crop marks or soil marks; normally soil marks can only occur where the land surface is ploughed at the present time. There are many parts of the world where, for a host of reasons, none of these indications of an ancient site may be expected. The uses of aerial photography are therefore limited by a number of factors to certain times and places.

Even in the areas where it is successfully used, it can only provide a certain amount of information, such as the shape and form of a site, its extent and perhaps a general indication as to its date and purpose. There are many other things, however, which it cannot tell the archaeologist but which it *is* possible to learn from walking over the site. Aerial photography, therefore, does not replace the field-walking; it is complementary to it, and certainly helps to define and limit the area to be covered and the questions the archaeologist will need to ask himself as he walks over the site.

What he will see and find is obviously determined by a range of different factors. On many prehistoric sites, there may only be a few scraps of badly weathered pottery and some handfuls of flint flakes, cores and implements. If bones are found, they may, partly depending on whether they are human or animal, indicate burials or rubbish deposits. On prehistoric sites in the Near-East, much greater amounts of pottery, stone and bone may be discovered, as well as traces of structures, not only as masses of tumbled stone or brick, but as recognisable wall foundations *in situ*. Building debris will include broken-up floors, roofing material, plaster, mortar and so on. These, with the occasional brooch, coin, pin and other small items, will enable the archaeologists to piece together a picture of the site and its history before he even considers excavation.

Probably the first thing he will establish is the age into which the site falls—Palaeolithic, Bronze Age, Iron Age or whatever—and within this broad category he will soon be able to date it a little more precisely. Of course, he may find it has been occupied in several different ages and periods. Breaks in the continuity of occupation are hard to recognise, but this is frequently possible where a sufficiently large amount of material has been collected. Recognition of the sudden, rather than the gradual, abandonment of a site also presents difficulties. Sometimes it may be possible to suggest the cause of such an event. For example, a mass of burnt debris, including a good many datable potsherds of a single period, would be reasonable grounds on which to postulate that a catastrophic fire had led to the site's abandonment. To this historical picture he is piecing together, the archaeologist can add some colour. The sort of debris he finds will tell him quite a lot about the sort of buildings that once stood here, in terms of their structure and interior treatment. Their purpose may be hinted at by metallurgical slags, fragments of votive figurines, broken quernstones, clay tablets and other finds. An archaeologist can, in fact, build up quite a detailed picture of a site just from a sackful of material dumped on his desk.

If he is a good archaeologist, however, he will not be satisfied just by collecting artifacts. Having found his site and made a preliminary examination, he will return with paper and pencil, measures and pegs, to record the position of what he finds. If he is going to excavate the site, he may well save himself a great deal of time and money in this way, for he will gain more detailed information as to the location of structures and other features. The scatter of building and occupation debris usually shows a pattern, revealing where the structures stood and giving some idea as to their alignment. Similarly, different concentrations of debris may indicate which were the main buildings and which the lesser ones, and even the approximate location of specific rooms.

It is at this point in the examination of a site that the archaeologist may most usefully employ methods of subterranean surveying. The first of these measures the resistance between two electrodes placed in the soil. This will reveal the presence of buried walls (higher resistance) and pits or ditches (lower resistance). The second measures magnetism in the soil, revealing areas of burnt clay and pits full of decayed organic material (higher magnetism). Using these methods, the archaeologist is able to pin down the location of many features on an ancient site before even putting spade to ground.

5. Have you found anything interesting?

Of all the questions posed by visitors to archaeological sites, this is probably the most common. Quite often it is followed by others in the same vein: 'Did you find any skeletons?', 'How many coins have you dug up?', 'What about brooches?' and so on. As these more specific questions clearly demonstrate, when the visitor asks if anything interesting has been found, he is thinking in terms of items of intrinsic value and immediate appeal. Most excavators realise this and give the site's 'vital statistics': ten coins, one cremation burial, and three bone pins, for example. Those who instead give a detailed summary of the site's history, or talk about some hitherto unrecognised local pottery fabric, simply reveal their own interests, which may be very different from those of the visitor. The archaeologist is intent on recovering information; the visitor wants to know about objects. To some extent the two requirements overlap, but very often they do not. The archaeologist will value, keep and study several categories of material which appear of no importance to the layman. Though often mystified by the excessive attention paid to pottery sherds, visitors may be inclined to give them the benefit of the doubt. So too with nails, flint flakes and blades. But tile fragments, pot boilers, pieces of clay daub and lumps of mortar are mostly regarded as just so much rubbish. Once one moves from man-made artifacts to natural remains—animal bones, mollusca, charcoal and soil samples—many visitors cannot understand why the archaeologist spends so much time and effort collecting and studying them.

Archaeologists need hardly be surprised at this. Indeed, until a decade or two ago, they themselves rarely kept snail shells and soil samples, and even today there are those who pay little attention to nails, tile fragments, mortars and similar materials. Yet a great deal of information can be derived from them, at least some of which will be of interest to the layman and the excavation visitor. The sight of an archaeologist carefully filling polythene bags with samples of the soil he is removing is but further confirmation to the visitor that archaeologists are, almost by definition, eccentric. After all, soil is soil—or is it? To begin with it is misleading to talk about 'soil' as if it were a single uniform material that will be dug through from surface down to bedrock; the archaeologists will collect samples not of soil but of soils. This plurality is very important. Natural causes and human activity lead to physical and chemical changes in soils; it is by studying these that the archaeologist—via the soil scientists—learns something of the natural processes and human activities to which his particular site has been subjected. Occasionally it may be possible to identify materials of which all visible trace has vanished. For example, American archaeologists excavating at Natrium, West Virginia, found a series of what appeared to be grave pits, though no bones could be found in them. Analysis of the soil, however, showed a very high phosphate concentration, indicating the former presence of bones subsequently destroyed by the acidity of the soil. More often a careful study of the physical composition of a soil reveals information about the weathering to which it has been subjected (and hence about climate), the sort of vegetation which grew in it (woodland, heath, grassland), and the way in which the soil was deposited (by water, wind or man). It can also indicate human interferences with the soil and the form they took. A few years ago, a Neolithic barrow at South Street, Avebury, in Wiltshire, was excavated. By studying the soils beneath it, which had been preserved there for 4,000–5,000 years, the excavator was able to identify two separate phases of agriculture, each followed by a fallow phase. As it happened, he was able to discover the marks left by the ancient plough (fig 4). Here, the study of the soils was producing information about the history of the site and of agriculture itself. Sometimes more is learned about the function of a site. It is possible, for example, to identify soils which have at one time been mixed with quantities of animal dung; this is obviously helpful in understanding

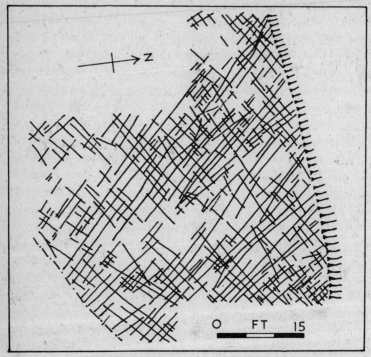

Fig 4: Plan of plough marks left by Neolithic man (*c* 3000 BC) in fields partly covered and thus preserved by a burial mound, at South Street, Avebury, Wiltshire. They represent initial cross-ploughing of land newly cleared for cultivation; the length of the longest marks suggests the plough was pulled— probably by an animal—rather than pushed. The activity represented by these marks was also evidenced by the soil profile and the small shells found within the soils. (*After J. Evans.*)

the uses to which various parts of an ancient farmyard were put. But valid conclusions on these lines can only be drawn where soil samples have been systematically taken and analysed.

A sample of soil will consist of more than just earth, of course. It will often contain tiny fragments of several sorts of material, such as charcoal, fibres, decayed mortar, small stones, pebbles and bones. In addition it may include small land mollusca (snails) and, in certain soils and under favourable conditions, pollen grains. The information provided by all these additional pieces of evidence is exhaustive. Pollen analysis alone reveals a great deal about ancient vegetation and climate, and can be invaluable in building a chronological framework for the past (see chapter 7). Here, only one of the materials, mollusca, can be discussed in any detail.

Land snails for the most part provide the same sort of information as soils; very often the joint evidence of mollusca and soils can be used to reconstruct a picture of the climate and vegetation of the ancient world. At the South Street long barrow at Avebury, for example, the archaeologist was able to confirm his interpretation of the soil profile by a study of the land mollusca, which showed a change from shade-loving species to grassland species (fig 5). Shells are also a useful source of material for carbon 14 dating of ancient deposits (see page 56), since shell absorbs comparatively large quantities of carbon dioxide—and hence carbon 14. In addition, some mollusca species are now being identified as *index species*, which only appear in certain places at certain times. *Helix aspersa*, for example, seems only to have been introduced into Britain in the Roman period.

Land mollusca have never been regarded as a major food-source as have marine mollusca (shellfish), which for the most part provide the archaeologist with information of a totally different sort. This is mainly of an economic nature, concerning shellfish utilised for food, and the relative popularity and

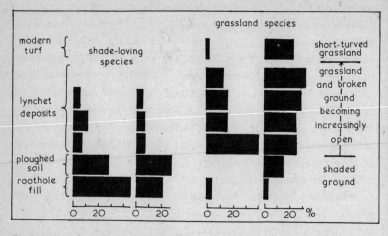

Fig 5: A simplified diagram to show how a comparative study of the snail shells found in successive deposits of soil can demonstrate changes which have taken place in the pattern of vegetation on a site. On the left, the four successive soil deposits are listed; on the right, the archaeologists interpretation of the evidence in terms of changes in vegetation. In the centre, four species of snails are represented—two of a shade-loving type and two of an open-grassland type. The numbers of shade-loving snails drop rapidly in the soil of the lynchet deposits, which accumulate at the edge of a cultivated field, and the number of grassland snails increases correspondingly. (*After J. Evans.*)

availability of the different species. Further information can be gathered by expert examination of the shells. It is possible, for example, to get some idea of the actual quantity of meat yielded by the different species—and to compare this with the volume of meat obtained from domesticated and wild animals— and also to learn something of the methods of collection. It can even be established at which season of the year the shells were gathered. All this information helps to create a much more accurate and detailed picture of early hunter-gatherer people living close to the sea.

More rarely, mollusca provides insights into other aspects of ancient life, such as the use of shells as necklace beads and simple decorations and their appearance as cult objects, as with the deposit of painted shells found alongside the famous Snake Goddess in the 'temple repositories' at Knossos in Crete. Conch shells seem to have been used in antiquity as both musical instruments and ornaments, but suitable specimens must have been difficult to obtain and may well have been objects of trade. Certainly conches discovered at some of the ceremonial centres of the Hopewellian culture of the American Mid-West must have been taken there from the coasts of Florida. Other sorts of shell and shellfish were also traded (fig 6). The masses of oyster shells in Romano-British towns and villas, for example, are indicative of a food-producing industry, and the shells of *murex trunculus*

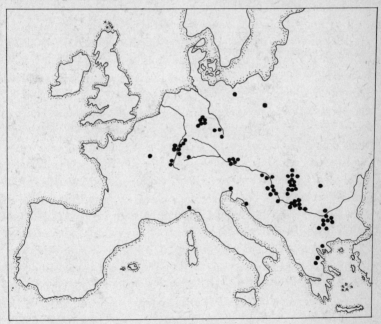

Fig 6: A map showing the distribution of *Spondylus* shells in ancient Europe. These were obtained from the Mediterranean and traded, particularly along the River Danube, deep into central Europe, where they were used by early Neolithic peoples to form necklaces. This is a particularly good example of shells being used as evidence for trading and trade routes which would be hard to document from other sources. (*After S. Piggott.*)

from sites around the Mediterranean are evidence of the pro-
longed popularity of purple dyes for cloth.

In contrast to this wide-ranging information which it is possible to derive from mullusca, evidence yielded by animal bones
may seem rather dull and limited. It is true that in the past they
were not infrequently used for ritual purposes—for figurines,
maces and, indirectly, in sacrificial ceremonies—as well as for
the manufacture of bone pins, awls, pendants, needles and
gaming pieces (fig 7). Most of these items are regarded as finds in
their own right. The mass of animal bones from an excavation,
however, will yield information concerned *almost* entirely with
subsistence economy.

A collection of such bones will initially indicate the range of
animals available to the occupants of a site. Old Stone Age sites
will reveal bones entirely of wild animals, while those of the
New Stone Age and later times will be largely of domesticated
animals, with smaller and varying quantities of wild ones which
were hunted. The next step is to try and place these animals in
order of numerical importance. One cannot, of course, assume
that, if forty cow bones and twenty sheep bones are found, there
were twice as many cows as sheep on the site. The zoologist must,
in fact, try to identify the minimum number of individual animals
present in any one single group of bones. Usually the number of
bones discovered is far greater than the number of individual
animals which the bones represent. For example, excavations
in 1968 inside the hillfort at Cadbury Congresbury, Somerset,
produced over 1,300 pig, cattle and sheep/goat bones, but only
230 individual animals could be *identified*. Once the minimum
number of individuals in a sample has been estimated, then the
basis of the animal husbandry can be established. Usually,
prehistoric and ancient farmers did not breed only cattle or only
sheep but indulged in mixed husbandry, and the animals were
bred for a variety of purposes. To clarify the relationship between the raising of cattle, sheep and pigs, and to understand

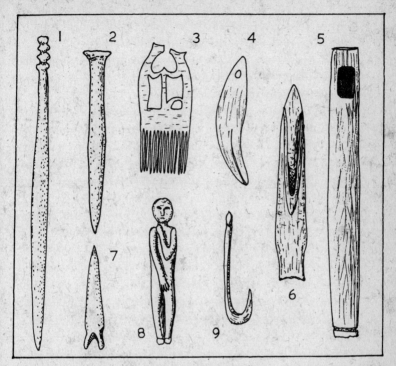

Fig 7: Artifacts made from bone and antlers by Iroquois Indians of New York State, USA: 1. notched awl; 2. punch; 3. comb; 4. pendant; 5. whistle; 6. spear-head; 7. arrowhead; 8. figurine; 9. fish-hook. The remarkable variety of the objects serves as a reminder to archaeologists of what may have been made by other prehistoric peoples out of wood, which would not have survived. (*After A. Parker.*)

something of the purposes for which the animals were raised, the zoologist must establish the age at which they were culled off and, if possible, what happened to their carcasses. Broadly speaking, where animals were kept to comparative old age it can be assumed they were reared for purposes other than meat production. This will usually mean that sheep were bred for wool; and cattle for use as draught animals, and for dairy products or hides. Where animals have been bred for meat, then it is important to establish what was consumed on the site and what was sold or traded elsewhere. In a native British farmstead of the Roman period, at Butcombe in Somerset, the absence of bones from the better joints of meat carries the suggestion that these were either being sold in a local market or perhaps were taken, as of right, by the landlord.

Information about other aspects of ancient life can also be gleaned from an examination of animal remains; although some of this tends towards the speculative, it is both interesting and unusual. For example, where it has been possible to estimate in what varying quantities animals were consumed, an assessment may be made of the amount of protein and vitamins constituting a people's diet. One may go even farther and suggest the sort of deficiency diseases from which communities may have suffered; where human skeletal material is available for study this can often be confirmed.

If the zoologist is provided with suitable samples of animal bone, he can tell the archaeologist a great deal. Fortunately the exchange of information is not entirely one way. Well stratified and dated skeletal remains of animals present the zoologist himself with much needed information. In some cases it may be a matter of identifying the point in time at which a particular species was introduced to a region. The domestic cat, for example, seems to have been introduced to Britain during the Roman period. An almost complete skeleton of such a cat sealed beneath a floor of c AD 300 in the Romano-British villa at Latimer, Buckinghamshire, was therefore an important find (plate 20), not only because it was well-dated but because it provided useful comparative material for the study of more fragmentary remains of early domesticated cats in Britain. A second important contribution which archaeology makes to zoology is the provision of information about the early development of animals and the effects of domestication upon them. Much has been learned about the development of modern breeds of cattle and

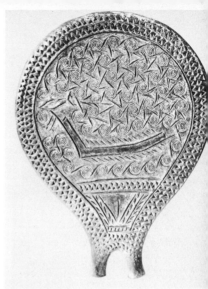

Plate 1 (*above left*): One of the store-rooms of the palace of Knossos, with huge *pithoi* (storage jars) against either wall. Sir Arthur Evan's discoveries included a magazine of almost two dozen such rooms.

Plate 2 (*above right*): A so-called 'frying pan' (*c* 2500–2000 BC) typical of a large group from the Cycladic Islands. It has a decoration of running spirals with a ship propelled by oarsmen, surrounded by a border of wedge-shaped incisions. On the base of the handle is a triangle with a line down the centre, which is thought to indicate that the object represents the female. It is not clear whether the objects are figurines or water mirrors.

Plate 3 (*below*): Rescue excavation in progress. Construction of the M5 in Somerset revealed a late Romano-British settlement. The scene, with machines, earth pushed to one side, mud and water, and the absence of carefully laid out and scrupulously tidy trenches, is typical of such rushed operations where time is at a premium.

Plate 4: Research excavation inside the Saxon Shore fort at Portchester, Hampshire, directed by Professor B. W. Cunliffe. In the centre are Roman cess-pits and a hearth; at the top are medieval drainage ditches and late Saxon rubbish pits. In complete contrast to Plate 3, the excavated areas are neat and tidy, the pace is unhurried and the site uncluttered. The archaeologist rather than the bulldozer dictates the speed and development of the work.

Plate 5: An old cottage in an advanced stage of decay. Once the windows and walls start to disintegrate and the roof collapses, plants quickly take root in the rotting debris on the floors.

Plate 6: A training excavation in progress on a Romano-British farmstead at Butcombe, Somerset. Here students are learning to wash, mark and sort pottery fresh from the dig. Others will be taught excavation techniques, surveying, drawing and recording,

Plate 7: An unusual 'hoard' of trade pots discovered at Horsetail Falls, Minnesota. They had been lost on the river bed when the boat in which they were being transported sank in the rapids. Archaeologists have begun to pay special attention to such potential danger spots as likely locations of whole shipments of early American trade goods in a state of preservation.

Plate 8: The *tell* of Jericho, a completely artificial hill resulting from almost continuous occupation of the site, from the ninth to the second millennium BC. Nomadic hunters, attracted first by the spring of fresh water, later began to settle here and slowly developed a community covering ten acres and defended by ditch, wall and towers. From this time onwards the continuous demolition and rebuilding of the mud-brick houses created a steady build-up of debris.

Plate 9: The robbed-out foundations of the tenth-century apse of the Old Minster at Winchester, one of many examples of stone robbing encountered during excavations there. The robbing in this case can be very precisely dated to AD 1093–4. Something of the complexity of excavating in a place that has been continuously occupied can be gathered from this photograph.

Plates 10, 11: The experimental chalk-cut ditch on Overton Down, Wiltshire, made in 1960 to study the changes which take place over periods of time in a ditch and in materials buried within the bank. *Plate 10:* the ditch as it was after a single winter's exposure. *Plate 11:* the ditch in 1964—the shape has undergone considerable modification and the bottom has already been buried. As turf and topsoil fall in and the sides become less steep, colonisation of plants and the formation of humus may occur.

Plate 12: The inside of a bakery in the Roman town of Pompeii. The excellent preservation of this and other buildings at Pompeii and nearby Herculaneum—both destroyed by the eruption of Vesuvius in AD 79—is due not only to the suddenness of the catastrophe but to their protection by the overlying volcanic deposits. The huge ovens and mills may be compared to their distant and more humble relatives in the Romano-British town at Gatcombe, Somerset (*Plate 30*).

Plate 13: A rescue excavation team recovering what they can of the plan of a mid-first-century Roman building, possibly the forum or market-place, discovered during construction work in London. In addition to the time limit, there is the tremendous complexity of levels resulting from long and continuous occupation.

Plate 14: Giant graders constructing a motorway in California uncovered a series of pits and postholes. Archaeologists are trying to excavate as much as possible of this Indian site before it is completely obliterated.

Plate 15: River erosion exposed the walls and floors of this Hellenistic-Roman settlement in Crete, enabling archaeologists to study the history of the site without excavating it. The vertical arrows on the photograph indicate the position of walls; the horizontal arrows mark the floor level. The river which was responsible for its initial discovery is also rapidly destroying the site by undercutting it during the winter months.

Plate 16: A severe storm in 1866 revealed the Neolithic village (*c* 2000 BC) of Skara Brae on the west coast of mainland Orkney. Excavation in the 1920s showed it to be a remarkable group of stone-built huts in which beds, hearths, cupboards and sideboards were all made of stone and therefore preserved.

Plate 17 (facing page, top): An aerial photograph of a 'shadow site'. Taken from an oblique angle in order to catch as much shadow as possible, it shows an extensive area of ancient fields which can be picked out by the shadow cast by their boundary banks. These fields on Rentwood Down, Wiltshire, are probably of Romano-British date. The same system can be traced as a series of soil marks in the ploughed field on the left. The low banks of the boundaries may be traceable at ground level, but the pattern they form can be more rapidly identified and studied from the air.

Plate 18 (facing page, bottom): An aerial photograph of 'crop marks' at Dorchester in Oxfordshire. A complex of ancient features is revealed; the dark lines represent buried ditches and pits belonging to several types of prehistoric site, mostly of the late Neolithic date (*c* 2000 BC). There is a long, narrow enclosure (*right of centre in the photograph*). Of the several circular, henge-type enclosures, there is an unusual example, at the bottom, surrounded by a rectangular ditch. Aerial photography can, with the right soil and climatic conditions, reveal such sites that are no longer visible at ground level.

Plate 19 (below): An aerial photograph of 'soil marks' at Ridgeway, Dorset, indicating a group of Bronze Age round barrows, which have been ploughed flat. At least six can be identified in the photograph, four of them linked together in a straight line. Similar barrow cemeteries were once a prominent feature of the English landscape, but deep ploughing has removed the characteristic mounds and very few remain undamaged. Aerial photography not only makes discoveries; it emphasises how many valuable archaeological sites have been destroyed.

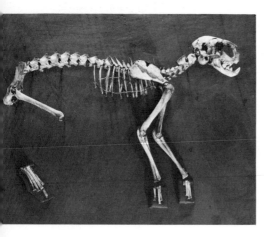

Plate 20: Skeleton of a domestic cat found beneath a floor in the Romano-British villa at Latimer, Buckinghamshire. Dated to *c* AD 300, it is a find of some importance to the zoologist, as closely dated and almost complete remains are rare. This particular cat proved on examination to have been between six months and a year old at death.

Plate 21: Romano-British pottery from south-west England: (*left*) two second-century vessels; (*extreme right*) early third-century beaker; (*behind*) fourth-century black jar; (*centre*) Samian bowl of glossy red pottery with moulded decoration on the outer face. The distinctive Samian pottery contrasts strongly with the 'coarse' local ware and is easily recognisable. It can be dated very closely, as it was produced by a small number of workshops in a few specialised centres in France. The work of each pottery is individually identifiable; the name of the potter-owner of the workshop concerned is also known in many cases.

Plate 22 (*right*): A fine example of a beaker from Eriswell, Suffolk.

Plate 23 (*below*): A food vessel, used as a cremation urn, from Bishop's Waltham, Hampshire. Vessels of these two types are the most common and identifiable artefacts associated with two separate but largely contemporary groups of people, now referred to as the Beaker and Food Vessel cultures, who inhabited parts of the British Isles *c* 2000–1500 BC. Other ancient people have been named after the site with which they were identified, e.g. Windmill Hill Culture, or the region where they seem to have concentrated, e.g. Wessex Culture.

Plate 24: This Mycenaean pictorial vase, showing a chariot pulled by two horses and carrying two men, was found in Cyprus with many more of its kind. Other vases of similar style and period have been discovered in Greece. Chemical analysis has established that the great majority were made in southern Greece and exported to Cyprus; this particular vase is thought to be one of the few produced in Cyprus.

Plates 25, 26: Two large clay vessels found in an Early Bronze Age settlement, *c* 2500 BC near Myrtos, southern Crete.
Plate 25: a spouted tub of the type used for olive oil separation.
Plate 26: a *pithoi,* or large jar, possibly used for storing the oil; it could also have held water or grain. Vessels like these throw light on both the pottery industry which produced them and the economy in which they were used.

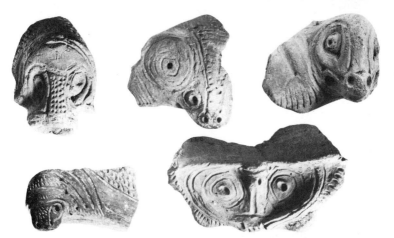

Plate 27: Modelled and decorated projections from early pottery bowls found at Puerto Hormiga, Panama. The various decorative techniques, distinctive sand-tempered fabric and associated fibre-tempered pottery all suggest that contacts existed with the south-east United States in the early third millennium BC.

Plate 28: In this tomb group found at Abydos in Egypt, all the objects are Egyptian except for the decorated vase in the centre. This is a well-known Minoan vase type painted in the 'Kamares' style and belonging to the Middle Minoan II period in Crete. It is one of several such vases exported to Egypt. A find like this is immensely important for the dating by historical means of prehistoric Aegean and even west European cultures. This tomb group contained two seals bearing the names of the pharaohs Sesostris III and Amenemmes III, whose reigns together covered the period *c* 1880–1800 BC. MMII in Crete—as well as other cultures in the Aegean and farther west which have links with it—can therefore be broadly dated to the nineteenth century BC.

Plate 29: A modern clay-lump wall at Yaxham, Norfolk. The clay-lump walls of medieval buildings in the area have long since disintegrated and are only recognisable by a tell-tale yellow stain in the soil. When mortared together and covered with a facing of plaster, the clay lumps make very substantial walls; however, as can be seen here, the plaster covering in time cracks and falls off. When completely exposed to the weather and left unmaintained, the wall will begin to disintegrate. This type of construction is the nearest equivalent in western Europe to the mud-brick walls of the Near East.

Plate 30: The function of these two adjacent structures (*c* AD 290) in the Romano-British town at Gatcombe, Somerset, was established by the presence of batteries of large baking ovens. Clearly the buildings were bakeries, not domestic dwellings. On the left, there is a large stone oven behind a quern or millstone platform and a small hearth.

Plate 31: An excavated tomb of *c* 2000 BC at Kamilari in southern Crete immediately after the removal of surface soil. A mass of large stone blocks has fallen from the upper parts of the wall, the remaining section of which showed a pronounced inward lean. This was achieved by corbelling—each course of stone slightly overlapping the one below. The fallen stone and the traces of corbelling are suggestive of a circular building which may once have been covered by a complete stone vault.

Plate 32: Many manhours were needed to excavate even this 'unassuming hollow' of a Saxon *grubenhaus* inside the defences of the Saxon Shore fort at Portchester, Hampshire. This small hut with sunken floor is typical of pagan Saxon settlements of the fifth century AD. Although architecturally simple, such huts may take up to fifty hours of careful work by modern excavation techniques. Further time will be required for the treatment of finds, and for recording the remains of the structure. Later come the longer processes of preserving the finds, studying and analysing material from the occupation layers and comparing it with that from other sites, and finally preparing the definitive report of the hut and its contents.

Plate 33: The remains of a timber building (late fourth or early fifth century) AD at Latimer, Buckinghamshire. Two parallel trenches, with straight sides and flat bottoms, are visible and, along their inner sides, four or five pairs of post-holes. This arrangement implies that sleeper-beams were laid in the trenches and that wall supports stood on them. The post-holes carried roof supports inwards to hold up the ridge.

Plate 34: The deep stratified deposits in the Purron Cave, Mexico, exemplify the kind of excavation work that can only be carried out by trained observers of minor differences in the colour and texture of soils. The dozens of levels, many of them floors with plant and animal remains on them, are visible in the photograph but were very difficult to recognise at the time of excavation. Each level had to be isolated and and then excavated without contamination from the levels above and below.

sheep from archaeological discoveries of the skeletal remains of their ancestors.

It should by now be apparent why archaeologists take such care to collect soils, mollusca and bones. Furthermore, what they learn from them is often the sort of information about the past which it might seem impossible to obtain. What weather did Britain experience in the Iron Age? What vegetation grew on the island of Crete in the Neolithic? What dietary deficiencies did the early American Indians suffer from? The answers have been supplied from a study of soils, mollusca and bones, together with other sources of evidence. To modern man these questions, and the collection of data to answer them, may seem pointless. He has little enough interest in his own natural environment, so it is hardly surprising that he should care even less about that of ancient man. But to the archaeologist, studying and trying to understand man in the past, the environment—which played a much greater role in his everyday life—is a key factor.

6. Why keep broken pieces of pottery?

Potsherds—fragments of broken pottery vessels—frequently attract the attention of visitors to archaeological sites, if only because of the vast quantities which are found. All but a very few New Stone Age communities made pottery and on sites of the Neolithic and later periods it usually forms by far the largest proportion of the finds. This is because a lot of pottery was used; it was easily broken and constantly needed replacement. For the archaeologist this fragility is one of pottery's two most important characteristics. The other is that, though fragile, it is remarkably resistant to destruction. Some poorly made pottery will crumble and disintegrate under adverse soil or weathering conditions and it *is* possible to grind pottery to a powder, but most of that broken in antiquity survives for many thousands of years.

Why are these two characteristics of pottery—fragility and indestructibility—so important to the archaeologist? First, both factors ensure that large quantities of pottery survive, and this makes its statistical study a valid and most useful approach. Secondly, the rapid turnover ensures that any changes of fashion —in shape, decoration, surface treatment, and so on—appear in rubbish deposits very shortly after they are introduced. The first of pottery's several roles, therefore, is to serve as a cultural indicator. Fashions in pottery shapes, decoration, and surface treatment reflect a people's artistic traditions, and perhaps other traditions too. It is thus possible to recognise communities which share a common tradition, by their use of similar styles and shapes of pottery. In this way the archaeologist is able to bring together dozens, even hundreds, of ancient communities and identify them as belonging to a single *culture*. He will not rely entirely on the evidence of pottery, of course, but will look for other common traditions—in architecture, weapons, tools, social organisation, funerary rites and so on. The basis of his cultural grouping, however, and the first indication of it, will almost invariably be the ceramic remains. The importance of pottery in this connection is demonstrated by the number of ancient cultures named after their most distinctive pottery products, for example, Beaker, Food Vessel and Funnel Beaker (plates 22, 23).

It follows that if a common culture amongst ancient communities can be recognised on the basis of the pottery used, then intrusions into that culture should be recognisable in the same way. Thus, pottery can be useful in identifying historical happenings or processes, such as invasion, migration and trade. In Greece, for example, the arrival of new settlers at the end of the third millennium BC is marked by the appearance of a very distinctive plain grey pottery, now referred to as Minyan ware. A little earlier, settlers were moving into Syria and Palestine where their presence is betrayed by their grooved and black polished pottery, which archaeologists have labelled Khirbet Kerak ware. In both cases, the pottery is so different from that in use previously that the arrival of new people seems certain. By careful study of pottery from different sites, and of the local material with which it was associated or which it superseded, it is often possible to trace the migratory route of a people and estimate how long the migration took. This has now been achieved for the very complex movements of the Beaker people between 2500 and 1500 BC in western and central Europe.

Pottery alone cannot be taken as final and irrevocable proof of an ancient migration; migrant peoples will reveal themselves in other ways too. Where anomalous pottery alone occurs, and that in use alongside large quantities of native pottery, then the archaeologist is more likely to be looking at evidence for ancient trade. Most pottery was not traded for its own sake, but principally as containers for other commodities. Nevertheless, the more attractive the packaging the better the sales and the higher the price, and many pottery vessels traded in antiquity were elaborately decorated. The Greek figured vases traded into Iron Age Italy were probably the most elaborate of all. Imported pottery consequently stands out very clearly from the local products and the archaeologist has little difficulty in recognising it. The glossy red, often highly decorated Samian ware produced in France in the first three centuries AD, for example, is easily distinguished in any assemblage of Romano-British pottery, even when British imitations of it are present (plate 21). Sometimes, however, imported pottery is not so readily identified; this frequently happens when dealing with trade within a single culture. Even then regional variations may be sufficiently clear for the identification of traded vessels, but this is not always the case. There is the classic example of the Mycenaean pictorial pottery found in Cyprus (plate 24). Was it made in Greece and exported to Cyprus, or vice versa? On the basis of style and motifs, a satisfactory answer has never been provided; but with the use of scientific aids archaeologists have obtained the information they sought. Examples of these pottery vessels were analysed for their chemical composition, and the results compared to similar analyses of clearly indigenous pots of various types from many locations in the Aegean and Cyprus. In this way it was possible to show that most of the pictorial vases were made in southern Greece and exported to Cyprus, although a few were made in Cyprus itself.

A stylistic analysis had been made of the Mycenaean pictorial pottery, even though an agreed solution was never reached by this method. But sometimes pottery may be so simple in style and decoration that it is not possible to use this approach. In such circumstances only a physical analysis of the pottery can provide evidence for trade. Instead of examining the chemical composition of the pottery, however, it may concentrate instead on its geological content—the tiny grits which have been included in the clay, whether deliberately or accidentally. Using this method of analysis, Dr Peacock has been able to demonstrate a remarkable trade, as long ago as 3000 BC, in pottery

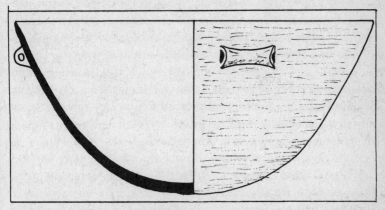

Fig 8: Diagram of a Neolithic bowl of a type known as Hembury F ware found in south-west England. These fine, thin-walled vessels with characteristic trumpet lugs were manufactured *c* 3000 BC. Examination of the grits in the clay from which they were made revealed they were the work of specialist potters living near the Lizard Head, Cornwall. The bowls were traded over distances of up to 200 miles. A complementary trade in axes made of Cornish greenstone was identified as a result of petrological examination of these implements. (*After S. Piggott.*)

which was made in southern Cornwall and distributed over distances of nearly 200 miles (fig 8). He has also provided evidence of other specialist potteries operating in the south-west nearly 3000 years later.

Such information is important, not only in demonstrating much wider trading contacts in the distant past than had previously been suspected, but also because it adds to the archaeologist's knowledge of the economic basis of a community. He begins to learn something about pottery production methods and the role of the potter in society. A lot of this information the archaeologist will be able to collect for himself, without referring to the geologist or chemist. A careful examination of pottery sherds will usually reveal whether a pot was coiled, made on a slow wheel or thrown on a fast wheel. This will give some indication as to whether the community possessed specialist potters—since fast wheels at least are usually the property of specialists—or if each household made its own pots. Dr Peacock's work on Cornish Neolithic pottery has demonstrated the dangers of assuming that handmade pottery is always the work of non-specialists. Unless the actual pottery works are found and excavated, as they sometimes are, any estimation of the size and importance of a pottery must be made on the known distribution and popularity of its products. This will usually mean a detailed examination— chemical, geological or of a more general kind—of the pottery's fabric. The archaeologist can often carry out this more general sort of examination himself. It consists of identifying the principal characteristics of the pottery's products: surface treatment (glazes, slips, washes), texture (hard, soft, sandy, smooth), inclusions (different types and size of stone particles) and basic colour of the material. Together these characteristics enable the archaeologist to identify different *fabrics*, a whole group of which he will build up into a *type fabric series*. By comparing these sample pieces with pottery sherds from other excavations he can begin to plot the distribution of the different fabrics and, where kilns have been excavated, to relate them to particular kilns. He will be able to take this one stage farther and organise a parallel *type form series*, showing which pottery shapes are made in the various fabrics. This may involve many years' work, but in the long-term it is worthwhile, producing a fascinating picture of how local potteries vied with each other for markets, the ways in which they specialised in certain types of vessels, and how sometimes one pottery prospered at the expense of another.

As well as supplying economic information about the industry itself, pottery also throws light on other parts of the economy. Since most of it was not made for its own sake, obviously something can be learnt from examining the functions which vessels were intended to perform. Much of it was simply kitchenware, but even pie-dishes, tankards and stew-pots provide some indication of food sources and the way in which they were utilised. Churns and strainer jugs are perhaps even more specific in this respect. On a more commercial footing, there were great vats and storage jars used in the production of oil, wine or dyes (plates 25, 26). Although it is difficult to distinguish an oil jar from a wine jar, other discoveries on the site, such as seeds, pips and presses, may suggest an identification. The quantity of such containers found in a house may be a useful pointer to the economic basis on which it prospered.

Useful and interesting as all this information may be, it is of little significance compared to pottery's major role in archaeology—the provision of a reliable chronological framework. In the study of the past, time is obviously a most important dimension; to bring order into chaos some sort of proved sequence is necessary. Once one reaches back beyond written history, the framework must be constructed around something other than historical events or calendars. The only material that occurs in large quantities almost universally is pottery, which will quickly register changes in fashions of decoration and design. It is thus the obvious material with which to construct a chronological framework.

The principle is simple enough. From a succession of levels on an archaeological site will come a series of groups of pottery. These will reveal differences one from the other, and each group will probably contain some types of pottery peculiar to that group. Distinctive pottery of this kind can be compared with that found in sequences on other nearby sites. In this way, limited sequences from several different sites can produce a longer sequence applicable to the whole region and into which future finds may be fitted. A simple diagram illustrates how this system works (fig 9). Parts of the sequence, or elements within it, may need to be clarified, for many changes in pottery styles

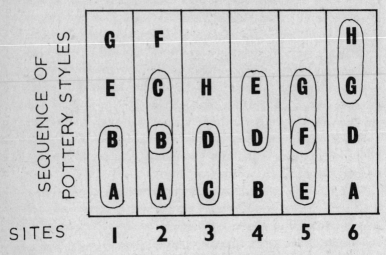

Fig 9: A simple diagram showing how a long pottery sequence can be built up from a series of short and incomplete sequences from many sites. The letters A to H represent eight different pottery styles, and the numbers 1 to 6 represent six excavated sites. The stratified pottery sequence from each site is represented by the vertical columns of letters. Although no single site produced more than three of the styles in the correct sequence, the whole sequence from A to H can be correctly identified due to the overlapping of the sequence on the other sites. The key areas of overlap, which allow the whole sequence to be established, are ringed.

and shapes took place over a long period of time rather than a short one. Where the archaeologist is faced with the problems of *trends* in pottery styles, he can often bring rhyme and reason into them by statistical analysis. It was possible, for example, to pick out trends in the Stone Age pottery of Knossos in this way (fig 10).

Once a regional framework has been established, two further steps may be taken. Within the region, the much rarer stratified

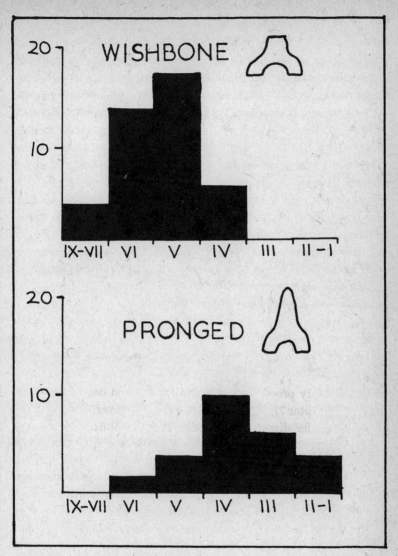

Fig 10: Two histograms showing trends in the wishbone and pronged handles used by Neolithic potters at Knossos in Crete. Numbers IX–I represent successive periods of occupation on the site; the vertical scale shows the quantity of each type of handle per 100 kilos of pottery in each period. This illustrates how each type rose to a peak of popularity and then lost favour; and also that pronged handles largely replaced wishbone ones from period IV onwards. (*After J. D. Evans.*)

finds of other types of artifact—bone pins, bronze tools or weapons, brooches, figurines etc—may be placed in the framework, because they will have been found alongside pottery whose position in the sequence is known. Beyond the region, links may be established with areas where different pottery styles were in use. This will depend to some extent on contact at the fringes of the regions; to some extent on the probably rare exchanges of pottery vessels as objects of trade or as gifts, and largely perhaps on the evidence of influences from one region to another affecting the development of pottery styles (plate 27). It was in this way, with a framework bolstered at various points by the scarcer evidence from other types of artifact, that during the 1920s Gordon Childe was able to construct a comprehensive chronological framework for prehistoric Europe.

Although Childe gave absolute dates to his framework, his chronological table was essentially a relative one; that is, it gave the *order* in which cultures succeeded one another rather than *when* the successions took place. Chronological frameworks based on pottery are still, in essence, relative ones, even though they can now be given reasonably precise time-scales based on several sorts of evidence (see chapter 7). Pottery itself, however, may in the future be able to offer direct evidence of absolute date. Two scientific techniques, both in the experimental stage, should eventually produce absolute dates from ceramic material. *Archaeomagnetic dating* will always be of limited application since it relies upon finding samples of pottery or other clay fired to a high temperature in antiquity and not disturbed since, even by the excavator. *Thermoluminescence* should be more widely applicable, although it is too lengthy a process to be used on large quantities of pottery and at present is subject to errors which are imperfectly understood. It seems likely that before long absolute dating will be added to the several important contributions which pottery makes to the study of the past.

7. How do you know how old it is?

Carbon 14 dating may be intriguing and tree-ring counting unbelievably precise, but I suspect that for many people they are poor substitutes for the 'mystique' of archaeological dating. It was not so long ago that the millions watching the TV programme, 'Animal, Vegetable and Mineral' gasped with astonishment and admiration every time Sir Mortimer Wheeler correctly gave the date of some ancient artifact, sometimes to within a few decades. How did he do it? What is the secret? This is what people want to know when they ask 'How do you know how old it is?' There is surprise, sometimes verging on disbelief, that an archaeologist can really distinguish between a piece of flower pot and a fragment of Roman pottery. That he can tell the difference between a potsherd made in the period AD 40–60 and another of AD 60–80 may seem little short of miraculous. How is it possible?

In the final analysis, archaeological dating depends on stratification or the accumulation of a succession of deposits which have some demonstrable relationship to each other. Study of the relationships between levels or deposits will reveal which is the earliest, the next earliest and so on. It follows that the same may be deduced about the various artifacts found within these deposits. On any single site, the sequence of deposits may well not be continuous or long, but (as already shown by fig 9) a long sequence can be built up by comparative studies between a whole group of sites. By studying and constantly handling the various materials making up these sequences, archaeologists come to know the forms, shapes, decorations and other features which characterise groups of artifacts at certain points in the sequence. They develop a 'feel' for pottery fabrics of different periods; it is largely this that enables them to distinguish in a second between flower pot and Roman pottery. If the archaeologist is asked what he means by 'feel' he may well have difficulty in giving a satisfactory answer, because it is something unconsciously acquired over a long period of time. His fingers have, in fact, become sensitive to differences in fabric, surface texture, weathering characteristics and so on of pottery of different periods.

It is fair to ask how the archaeologist constructs his chronological framework when confronted by the remains of Palaeolithic or Mesolithic man, who did not have the use of pottery. As long as deposits can be found in stratified sequences and yield fair quantities of artifacts, such as flint and bone implements, the system still works, though it becomes perhaps a little less precise. Changes in the type and form of stone implements, as well as in the technique of stoneworking, make it possible to recognise products of different periods. Where such objects are found in small quantities, and in strata isolated from others containing human artifacts, then the archaeologist has to resort to the evidence of natural sequences. For example, since the mid-nineteenth century, remains of early man have been placed in the time-scale on the evidence of the geological deposits in which they were found. The more precise vegetational sequence has now been recognised, its general development being traced by the study of pollen grains. Those shed by living plants are remarkably tough and under suitable soil conditions will survive for millennia. The botanist can identify the different genera, or families, of plants by their distinctive pollen grains; by comparing the quantities of each genera present in a sample of soil from an ancient site, he can draw up quite an accurate picture of the vegetation on and around the site at the time the particular soil was on the surface. The pattern of vegetation has changed

many times in the course of thousands of years; it is now possible to divide the past into a number of *vegetation zones*, each
characterised by a certain pattern of vegetation (fig 11). If,
therefore, an archaeologist can obtain a soil sample with pollen
grains, associated with an isolated deposit or even a stray find,

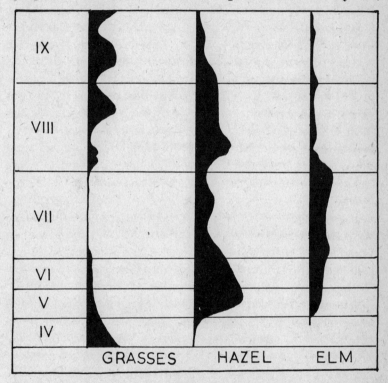

Fig 11: A simplified diagram illustrating part of the sequence of vegetation in
Jutland since the last Ice Age, as determined by pollen analysis. The growth
pattern of only three genera—grasses, hazel and elm—are shown here, and the
first three vegetation zones (periods) are omitted. If, for example, a soil
sample contained relatively large quantities of elm pollen, moderate amounts
of hazel pollen and little or no grass pollen, it could be placed in zone VII. On
the other hand, large quantities of grass pollen, small amounts of hazel and very
little elm would place the sample in zone IX. Any artifacts found in the stratum
from which the sample was taken could be placed in the same zone as the
sample.

he can place the deposit or find into one of these zones; in other words, he can date it.

Nevertheless, to say simply that an artifact dates to zone 5 or zone 6 is not entirely satisfactory, particularly to the layman. All the dating methods so far mentioned give relative, as opposed to absolute, dates. This is not to say that relative dating is unimportant or has no value. It is still the essence of understanding the past, but without an accompanying absolute chronology it is incomplete. The great value of absolute dating is that it conveys an idea of tempo in the development of civilisation. Man has not developed at the same speed throughout history nor indeed throughout the world. To understand the way in which a civilisation developed it is essential to recognise changes in the speed of development. The archaeologist needs to know not just that a people went through a certain stage but whether it took fifty or five hundred years for them to do so.

Until the advancement of scientific methods of absolute dating, the prehistoric archaeologist was entirely dependent on converting his relative chronologies into absolute ones. For example, he could not give absolute dates for pre-Columbian remains in the Americas, or for pre-European remains in the Antipodes because these civilisations could not be fitted into the relative chronologies for Europe, Asia and northern Africa, since there were no recognisable links between them. With no scientific dating methods to resort to, the prehistoric archaeologist had but one source of absolute dates: the historical civilisations of the Near East—Egypt, Mesopotamia, Syria, Palestine and Turkey. This meant that the period of absolute dating could not reach back before about 3000 BC. For the period thereafter it was a matter of demonstrating links between cultures which were historically dated in Egypt, the Levant or Mesopotamia and those of prehistoric peoples which spread out beyond them.

These links could take several forms; for the archaeologist, trade was the most obvious and perhaps the most reliable (plate 28). Where goods of known date were imported from Egypt or the Levant by prehistoric peoples, then a date could be given to the native products with which they were associated when found by the archaeologist. Sometimes these native people would have traded with other prehistoric peoples having no direct contact with Egypt or the Levant. In this way, these people too might be given absolute dates, and so on along a whole chain of connections until dates were provided for the prehistoric cultures of western and northern Europe at one end of the chain and ancient India at the other. It has not always been possible to demonstrate a series of trading links, however; many of the links in the chain are based on less certain connections, open to more subjective interpretation. These may take the form of external influences on the development of indigenous ceramics, architecture, metalwork and so on. This sort of chronology is essentially relative and absolute dates applied to it can be, and have been shown to be, seriously in error. Obviously all sorts of factors can lead to such errors, but a general rule can be formulated by which to assess the value of absolute dates obtained by this method. The greater the time and distance between the prehistoric culture being dated and the historic civilisation providing the basis of the dating, the more tenuous are the links—and the less reliable are the dates—established.

There are some cultures which are neither prehistoric nor historic. Some of these, on the verge of becoming historic and writing their own records, are called protohistoric cultures; while others stand on the fringe of history, sometimes written about by historical neighbours and occasionally conquered by them. The classic example, of course, is Britain under the Romans. The archaeologist is better off when faced with this sort of situation than with entirely prehistoric peoples, but he

nevertheless has difficulties in building a satisfactory absolute
chronology. He will usually have a bare skeleton of historical
information on which to build, such as a few important battles,
occasional rebellions and imperial visits to the conquered ter-
ritory. In the case of Roman Britain, it is known that the invasion took place in AD 43, that Boudicca rebelled in AD 60–1
and that Severus came to England in AD 205 and died at York in
AD 211. Some of these dates provide the framework for the
history of the province, but others have an additional value, for
they are associated with events which can be recognised in the
archaeological record. For example, Boudicca's destruction of
Colchester, London and St Albans has been clearly identified on
many occasions during excavations (fig 12). Obviously, the
mass of pottery and other artifacts found in these destruction
deposits can be dated very closely indeed—to AD 60–1, in fact.
Others can be closely dated on the evidence of inscriptions,
which often record the foundation or completion of a certain
building, or perhaps its repair after partial destruction. Although
the Romans did not inscribe the date in so many years AD, they
did something almost as useful by recording the number of
times the emperor had held the consulship and other titles at the
time the inscription was cut. This often indicates the date of the
inscription to within a year or two, and this in turn dates pottery and other items discovered in the foundation material or in
the debris resulting from repair work. Finally, coinage is an
important factor in dating Romano-British deposits. From the
mint-marks on the coins relatively close dating of their time of
issue can be established—some emperors being very short-lived,
in any case. Where a sufficient number of coins can be found in a
single deposit, further dating evidence is provided for pottery
and other artifacts. Single coins, however, can be very misleading indeed; some stay in circulation for many decades, or
even longer, after they are minted. These various sources of
historical dating for Romano-British deposits are the backbone

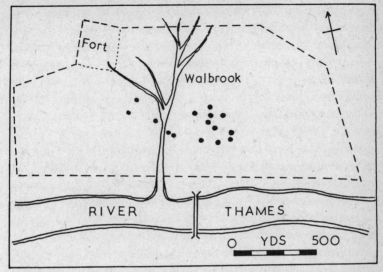

Fig 12: Plan of Roman London showing the sites of destruction deposits of the Boudiccan revolt. The dotted line indicates the position of the later Roman wall. Boudicca's destruction of Londinium, AD 60–1, left thick deposits of fire debris which have helped archaeologists in two ways. Because the event itself is precisely dated from historical sources, pottery and other artifacts found in the destruction deposits can also be given an accurate date. Also the plotting of these deposits on a map of Roman London shows both the siting and the approximate size of Londinium in AD 60–1, only seventeen years after the Romans landed at Richborough. (*After R. Merrifield.*)

of the absolute chronology of Roman Britain. By using pottery, brooches and other items found in historically dated deposits to build up absolutely dated sequences of these artifacts, it is possible to date deposits which themselves contain no direct clues to their absolute date.

This method of dating works so well with regard to Roman Britain, and indeed in similar situations elsewhere, that it has not been superseded by any of the scientific methods of dating. It is both more precise and more reliable than carbon 14 dating; and, unlike tree-ring dating, which is very precise indeed, it can be widely applied regardless of climate and suffers from no

shortage of samples, pottery being the basis of it. Carbon 14 and
other scientific methods of dating, however, are invaluable for
the prehistoric periods and have revolutionised the archaeologist's ideas about the absolute chronology of the prehistoric
culture sequence throughout the world. These scientific methods
have three great attractions. Firstly, they are objective.
While the results may be variously interpreted by the archaeologists, they derive from calculations based on observed
scientific facts and measurements made under carefully controlled conditions. Carbon 14 dating, for example, is based on the
fact that radioactive particles of C14 absorbed by a living
organism begin to disintegrate at a known, constant rate when
the organism dies. Secondly, scientific methods of dating can
be applied to isolated cultural sequences, for they do not rely on
establishing links with historical civilisations. Until the introduction of C14 dating, for example, it was impossible to do
more than guess at the dates of the prehistoric cultures who
inhabited the American continent before the arrival of the first
Europeans. A whole sequence of dates is now being built up and
in some areas, such as the Tehuacan valley of Mexico, there is a
complete series of a hundred dates covering ancient societies
from soon after 10 000 BC down to the arrival of the Spaniards.
The third attraction of the scientific means of dating is that they
have greatly extended the span of human history for which an
absolute chronology can be built. In Mesopotamia, where the
earliest written documents could carry historical dating just
beyond 3000 BC, there is now a dated sequence stretching back
to at least 8000 BC—its span of dated history has been doubled!
The same is true of many prehistoric societies who were remote
from—but until recently dated by—the early historical civilisations. Many archaeological equations between prehistoric
Europe and the civilisations of the Near East have now been
shown to be false, and the resulting chronologies considerably in
error.

To take the most obvious example, the beginning of farming in some parts of Europe and the Near East has been moved back in time, mainly on the evidence of C14 dates, by as much

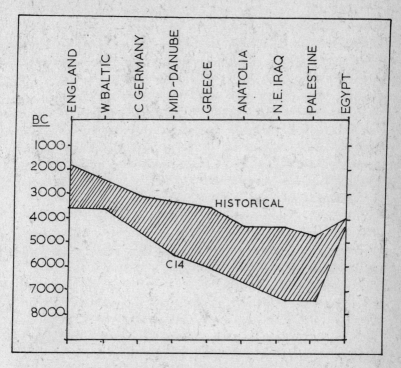

Fig 13: A simple graph of the beginnings of farming in Europe and the Near East, showing the difference in the dates estimated by historical means and those obtained by carbon 14 dating. It illustrates the tremendous impact of C14 dating, which pushed back by many millennia the beginning of farming in several areas. Since 1950, when C14 dating began, the discovery of previously unknown Neolithic cultures in Turkey, northern Iraq and Palestine has tended to increase the discrepancy between C14 and historical dating to a greater degree than in other areas. (*Based on J. G. D. Clark*.)

as 3000 years (fig 13). Changes of this magnitude involve more than a simple alteration of dates; they offer entirely new perspectives in prehistory and the development of civilisation. A mental adjustment is needed in order to think of the New Stone Age as proceeding at a totally different tempo to that previously accorded to it. Further changes may be in store, for various factors which influence the carbon 14 dates obtained from ancient organic materials are gradually being discovered and understood. Tree-ring counting, which is remarkably precise, is playing a particularly important role in correcting and bringing more precision to C14 dating. Indeed, an added attraction of scientific methods of dating is the diversity of materials from which absolute dates can be extracted. The archaeologist can now obtain absolute dates from wood and plant remains (including pollen), bone, shell, clay and obsidian. Few sites will not yield at least one of these sources of dating evidence. It will be some years before many of the various methods utilising these materials will be entirely reliable and accurate, and probably even longer before they are economical enough to be employed for every excavation. But, by the end of this century, much of the archaeologist's concern over timescales will probably have been obviated by the sciences.

The use of carbon 14 and the other scientific dating techniques is expanding rapidly, and their future potential is great indeed. The majority of excavations, however, are still dated by archaeological methods, partly for reasons of finance and partly because in many cases this evidence is still the more precise. Certainly when an excavator in the field tells a visitor that the long barrow he is excavating dates to c 3000 BC, it should not be assumed he has a geiger counter in his hut and sits there running off carbon 14 determinations. Even if he has samples from his site, he will only get dates from them, via the laboratory, several months after the excavation has taken place. The date he gives the visitor, though it may in the final analysis depend on C14 dates for other comparable long barrows, will have been arrived at through the usual processes of archaeological dating. He will have assessed the significance of the pottery and other artifacts he has found and of the barrow itself, and related them to finds from barrows elsewhere. In other words, he will have built up in his mind a relative chronology for his own particular barrow. It is unlikely that scientific techniques will ever replace this part of the 'mystique' of archaeological dating.

8. What was it?

While many visitors may not show much interest in the problems of archaeological interpretation, they do want to know what the visible physical remains on the site—walls, floors, post-holes and so on—represent. They want to find out what they are looking at. The amount of information which the archaeologist can provide usually surprises them and leaves them sceptical. How, on the basis of a few post-holes and scraps of wall foundation, can a building be reconstructed to the roof and the interior decoration be described in detail? Obviously, since each structure will differ as to its function and original appearance, no general answer can be given to the question, 'What was it?' Similarly, the evidence on which function and appearance are identified will vary from one site to another, but it may be helpful to explain how an archaeologist approaches the reconstruction of an ancient building and the sort of evidence he uses.

In many ways the interpretation of architectural remains is one of the easier tasks facing the archaeologist when he begins to sort out what his evidence means. He is, after all, dealing with primary evidence—the physical remains of the structures themselves. Nevertheless, there are other factors to be considered, which together constitute the environment in which the buildings existed. These climatic, technological and social conditions will have helped to determine the sort of structures erected by an ancient people and the way in which they set about it. For example, buildings were unlikely to be made of timber in a region where trees were scarce but stone was abundant; and people who could not read or write would not build libraries. The archaeologist must therefore know something of the contemporary climate, availability of raw materials, and the social and technological development of the people concerned. He must also be familiar with other buildings, if they have been excavated, belonging to the same period and culture as the structures he is investigating.

Before he reaches the stage of planning the architectural remains on his site, the archaeologist will usually have decided what is and what is not evidence for ancient structures. Sometimes this is a perfectly straightforward task, but it can be a difficult one, requiring considerable experience and insight. In the Near East, for example, mud-plaster floors and decayed mud-brick are only two of many structural features which may be missed altogether by an inexperienced excavator. In western Europe similar problems may arise in tracing the lines of long-since dissolved clay-lump walls, now represented by little more than a yellow stain in the soil (plate 29). Where buildings with stone foundations are concerned, there is obviously a much better chance of physical remains surviving in easily recognisable form. However, the activities of later generations who robbed the ancient walls in order to re-use the stone may mean that an archaeologist will not infrequently find a *robber trench* where once stood a solid stone wall (plate 9). In addition, the excavator of stone buildings will need to examine very carefully and plot in on his plans large amounts of stone rubble, which is evidence of the ancient structure just as much as are the surviving fragments of wall and floor.

All the structural features will be included in the excavator's detailed plan of the architectural remains, from which he will begin to interpret his evidence in terms of buildings. The completed plan will represent the sum total of evidence for structures discovered on the site *in situ*. There will be other evidence which was not found in the place where it originally stood. For example, on an Iron Age site in western Europe, there is often

plenty of burnt clay daub lying about. On a Roman site, tiles,
plaster, pieces of flooring, perhaps even a fragment of stone
lintel or column, will usually be scattered around and inside the
building. With all such evidence assembled in the form of plans,
drawings and photographs, interpretation can begin. (A certain
amount of interpretation in fact takes place during the excavations but this is preliminary and subject to alteration later.)

The first stage of interpretation must be in terms of history;
that is the whole sequence of structural remains must be
established and drawings made of the remains of each individual
phase. This is essential, for the master plan will show the sum
total of remains. In this respect it may be misleading, as can
be seen by comparing the master plan of a small Roman villa
with the excavator's interpretation of it in terms of a sequence
of structures (fig 14). At no time were all the walls on the master
plan in use together and, in this sense, it shows a non-existent
building. The basis of the method by which the excavator
establishes his sequence and decides which walls and floors were
contemporary is *stratification*. In other words, the archaeologist
must sort out which floors are cut through by which walls;
which floors run up to the walls and which overlie the grubbed-
out foundations of other walls, and so on (fig 15). Obviously,
this exercise is much easier when dealing with stone walls and
substantial floors than with structures represented by a mass of
post-holes and at best a sequence of earth floors; but the
principles remain the same.

Having established the sequence of structures, the archaeologist can now tackle each building individually. Since very
rarely will he find more than the foundations, the first problem
he will have to consider is the nature of the superstructure. The
foundations will give him some idea as to what this will have
been like. For example, post-holes or sleeper trenches—for
the placing of horizontal wooden beams—clearly imply a timber framework; while massive stone foundations are unlikely

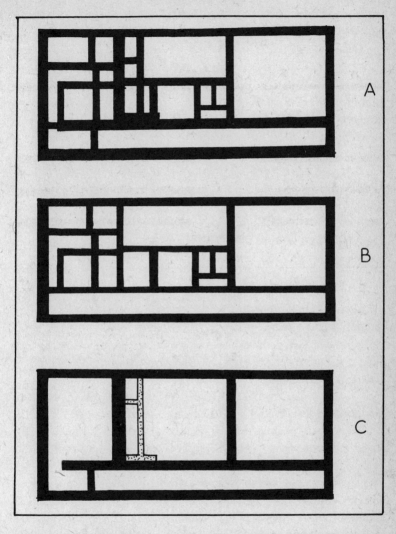

Fig 14: The Romano-British villa at Saunderton, Buckinghamshire. A: the master plan of the building, showing all the walls discovered during excavation. B–C: the historical interpretation of the plan, revealing a sequence of three buildings, none of which are identical to the building in A. In this sense, the master plan shows a structure which never existed. (*After D. Ashcroft.*)

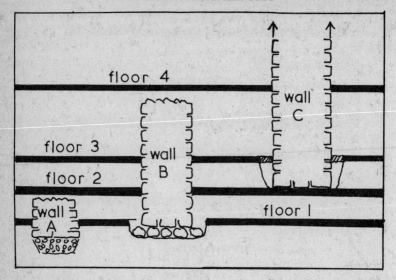

Fig 15: Diagram illustrating the interpretation of an excavated building in terms of its architectural history. The earliest remains are floor 1 and wall A, which are associated with each other. Wall B is cut into the surface of floor 1, and wall A is overlain by floor 2. Both wall A and floor 1 therefore went out of use when floor 2 and wall B were built. Subsequently the floor was renewed (floor 3) while wall B remained in use. Wall C was then built, cutting through floor 3 to rest its foundations on floor 2 ; but floor 3 remained in use, the foundation trench for wall C being covered over by a patch. Only later was wall B demolished and floor 3 replaced by floor 4.

to have carried a light timber superstructure. But what of slighter stone foundations? These could have been used as nothing more than a sill for a wooden superstructure; the building might have been half-timbered or the walls built in stone up to the eaves. There are several indications which can be sought to solve this problem. The amount and extent of rubble is one obvious clue (fig 16). Another is the discovery of wall plaster or daub carrying impressions of hurdling or wattle. Primary evidence of roofing materials often survives in the form of tiles or slates, thick lumps of plaster bearing impressions of hurdling or wooden beams, charred fragments of beams or, in the case of stone vaulting, rows of collapsed stones (plate 31). The shape of the roof will be suggested by the shape of the building and the position of the roof supports inside it (plate 33). Roofing materials will also be borne in mind, since those of lighter weight obviously allow greater spans and introduce more flexibility—in this sense—into the arrangement of the roof supports. In the final analysis, this process of reconstructing the shell of the building will prompt the archaeologist to ask himself three questions: 'What do the surviving remains sug-

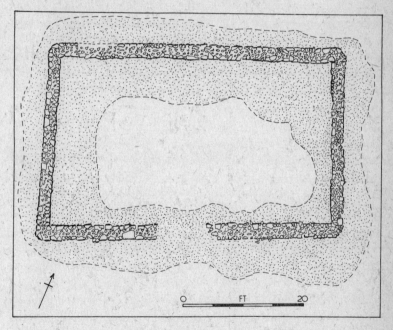

Fig 16: Plan of a farm building in the native settlement at Butcombe, Somerset, showing the extent of the rubble which had tumbled or been dislodged from the walls. The small amount of tumble suggests that these could never have been much higher than the four courses preserved at the north-east corner, and that the building was largely of timber, erected on stone footings. The structure and the enclosure in which it stands date to *c* AD 270–350, but overlie a succession of earlier structures dating back to perhaps the fifth century BC. (*After P. J. Fowler.*)

gest?', 'Is there anything missing which would survive if my hypothesis is correct?', and 'Was the method and arrangement I postulated structurally sound and technologically possible for the people who constructed the building?'

From the shell, the archaeologist moves to the fittings. Where were the doorways? Often they will be clearly marked by thresholds, sockets, surviving fragments of jambs, different spacing of the wall supports or an outside path leading to them. Even where all of these are absent, other clues can be sought. An earth, clay or even plaster floor, for example, will usually reveal much more wear near doorways than elsewhere. If living conditions were squalid and occupation debris collected on the floor, there will usually be a much thinner deposit by the doorway than in the rest of the room, since it is unlikely that anyone would block the entrance to his living room with rubbish. On the other hand, the number of housewives of ancient times who tossed their rubbish just outside their open door is remarkable—and very useful as these deposits are another indication of the vicinity of a doorway. The subdivision of the building into rooms or areas may not be as apparent as it is in a Roman villa or a Mesopotamian town house. In prehistoric timber huts, interior partitions may have consisted of nothing more than skins hung from rafters, leaving no visible remains or at best thin wattle walls which might be traceable in the form of stake-holes in the floor. In such circumstances, these partitions are suggested by differences in the wear and nature of the floor, the distribution of small finds and the spread of occupation debris, as well as from more obvious features like hearths and ovens. Although furniture rarely survives (plate 16) the position of beds, cupboards, and so on can sometimes be fixed by very regularly shaped areas of floor where occupation debris and wear are absent.

The identification of two-storey buildings is often very difficult. Except for substantial flights of stone steps, stairs seldom survive; but wooden ones can sometimes be identified where stair-wells—usually small square or oblong rooms with a strong supporting cross wall or central pier—can be recognised. More frequently, however, the only evidence for a second storey is where the debris and artifacts from the upper floor are found lying on the collapsed ceiling material of the room below. Many of the famous Linear B tablets from the Minoan palace of Knossos were found in this situation.

Little has so far been said about identifying the function of a building; in most cases this presents little difficulty (plate 30). If it is not revealed by the plan of the building and its fittings, then very often the answer can be found in the material inside and around it. The most frequent exceptions to this rule are buildings which have served a ritual function. Here, the problem is not only to identify with certainty the religious nature of the building, but also to establish whether it was used privately or communally. In most ancient societies, cult furniture, such as cult figures, altars, offering tables, figurines, sacrificial deposits, lamps and ritual pits, is remarkably uniform, so that most shrines can easily be identified as such. The point at which this or any other identification of function is made will vary from site to site and structure to structure. A provisional identification of the function of a building will have been arrived at by most excavators while they are digging it, and few approach the task of interpretation without a reasonably clear idea of what they think it was used for. This may seem to be putting the cart before the horse; in fact, the function of a building will often determine not only its interior decoration and fittings but also, to varying degrees, its design and construction.

From this brief description of the way an archaeologist approaches the interpretation of structural remains, it should be possible to understand the basis of all archaeological interpretation. The secret of successful and correct deduction lies largely, but not entirely, in the collection of evidence. The more information that the archaeologist can acquire from his observations in the field and in the study, and the more that his array of specialists can extract from the various groups of material, the better will be his chances of providing a correct and comprehensive re-construction of his site in antiquity. Similarly, the greater his experience and knowledge of the human and natural environment of the site, the more accurate and detailed will be his reconstruction of it in all its aspects. But beyond knowledge and information lies something more—a mixture of intuition and a controlled use of the imagination. Often it is only by the combined use of all these resources that the archaeologist can answer the question 'What was it?'

9. Why is excavation so slow?

At first sight this might seem to be a thinly veiled request for a time and motion study of archaeologists and excavations. The comment, so often expressed by onlookers, that labourers could do it all so much more quickly carries implicit questions: 'Why is it necessary to remove the soil so carefully?'; 'Why the need for expertise and skill?' and, in the final analysis, 'Why archaeologists? Cannot anyone expose walls and floors and collect coins and pottery?' The simple answer is that anyone can, but he will be left with walls, floors and pottery and little else. The amount of information he will gather will be negligible and, in the long term, so too will be the sense of satisfaction. Though the initial thrill of discovery will remain, the deeper rewards of detection and deduction, interpretation and reconstruction will be lost.

It should by now be understood why it is that excavation must be left in the hands of skilled and trained specialists. Only by training and experience do excavators know what to look for and what is significant. Only a trained and experienced eye will recognise the importance, or even the existence, of slight changes in the colour or texture of the soil (plate 34). These may represent almost anything from a scrap of rotted waste leather to the post-holes and sleeper-trenches of a very large building. It seems most unlikely that labourers would have discovered the great Saxon palace at Cheddar, whose presence was detected in this way (fig 17).

The amount of time an archaeologist spends on excavating work would be much less than it is, however, if he were only

concerned with the actual digging of the site. But he is trained
not only to excavate and observe, he must also record. Excavation, as has been pointed out, is by nature destructive;
once a site has been excavated then it is gone for good, and the
work cannot be repeated. For this reason a complete and accurate record of his discoveries is as important as the skilled use
of the best and latest excavation and preservation techniques.

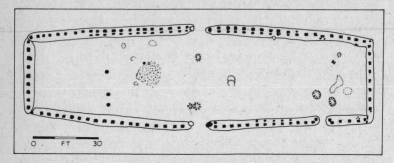

Fig 17: Diagram of a Saxon long hall at Cheddar, Somerset, of which no
physical remains survived for the excavators to find. It was traced only by
changes in the colour and texture of the soil at points where there had once
been post-sockets and the trench in which they were placed. It had been a
substantial building, about 80 ft long and made entirely of timber; it is thought
to date to the ninth century. Excavation of such sites requires not only care and
expertise but a great deal of time. (*After P. A. Rahtz.*)

This will mean that during his work on a site the archaeologist
will make dozens, perhaps hundreds, of plans, sections and
sketches, each requiring many measurements to be made. Each
post-hole, for example, is usually drawn both in plan and in
profile. A single section may have several dozen individual
levels in it, each of which has to be measured in at short,
regular intervals. In addition, both the small finds and the
general finds are carefully recorded—the small finds three-
dimensionally—notebooks full of on-the-spot observations are
made and hundreds of photographs taken. All this requires a
great deal of time, but if it is done properly the site can be

reinterpreted any time in the future. In this respect the excavation reports of Pitt-Rivers, who excavated widely on Cranborne Chase, Wiltshire, in the late nineteenth century are adjudged to be remarkable. Sixty years afterwards, Professor Hawkes was able to re-interpret the sites in such detail that it might be called a case of 're-excavation on paper'. Of course, Pitt-Rivers did not keep soil samples or mollusca, nor did he collect pollen grains; in the 1880s no one realised that so much information could be obtained from such evidence. But the modern archaeologist does know, and in consequence takes his soil samples and collects his snail shells, along with samples of charcoal and mortar and others, for archaeomagnetic or C14 dating. This not only takes time but demands considerable knowledge of what constitutes a good sample for each technique, and the correct methods of individual collection and storage. This work cannot be left to the untrained excavator, who may know his prehistory and excavating techniques but will usually be unaware of the intricacies of collecting samples. Archaeology today is both too broad and too specialised to be a suitable field of activity for either the dilettante or the single-minded 'digger' bent on 'finding things'.

What the public often fails to realise is that, although the period of excavation may seem long to them, it is in fact but a small fraction of the total amount of time an archaeologist will spend in investigating his site. As has already been explained, a considerable amount of preparatory work needs to be done before he even begins excavating. A great deal more work, in terms of study, preservation and interpretation, must be carried out when the excavation is over, before he can commence the long task of writing his final report. Depending on the type of site the archaeologist has excavated, large quantities of flintwork, pottery, animal bones and other materials will have to be washed, sorted perhaps as many as three or four times, and then carefully studied in detail. Drawings must be made of many of these items, and for some of them the archaeologist will try to find parallels from other excavations which may throw additional light on the history or the importance of his own site. While he is thus engaged on the collections of human artifacts, other specialists will be working on the soil samples, pollen grains, animal bones, plant remains and other materials recovered. A conservationist will begin the task of permanently preserving many of the finds which had only received 'first aid' at the time of discovery. Finally, there is the writing and publishing of a definitive report on the excavation and its results. This will involve many months of careful marshalling of the evidence, and of the provision of drawings and photographs to illustrate it. How long does all this take? A few years ago, Professor Barry Cunliffe estimated the amount of man hours spent by himself and his colleagues on the excavation, subsequent study and interpretation of a Saxon *grubenhaus*, or hut, at Portchester Castle in Hampshire. The *grubenhaus*, like others of its kind, survived as little more than 'an unassuming hollow'—a mere 10 sq m of excavation (plate 32). Even so, eighty-three hours were required for excavating and recording it, and for the finds from it to receive preliminary treatment. With the work of study, interpretation and publication still unfinished at the time of Professor Cunliffe's estimate, another 165 hours had already been devoted to post-excavation work on the hut and its contents.

Seen in this light, and bearing in mind the amount of information which the skilled and careful archaeologist will wring from even the most unproductive sites, excavations lasting two, four or even eight or ten weeks may perhaps be regarded more favourably. For every week of excavation—and of possible inconvenience to a farmer, a contractor, a builder or to the public in general—the archaeologist will, for many more weeks, strive to extract the maximum amount of information from his evidence. In time the outcome of his endeavours will give mu-

seum staff the opportunity to prepare new displays to feed back
to the public the results of his many months of excavation and
study. Some of the more outstanding discoveries may feature
in television programmes, and the new information will appear
in book form on the shelves of public libraries. People who
visited the excavations in the field may see these displays,
films and books, and to the questions they asked then—and
around which this book has been written—they will begin to
add others. Who were the people who lived on this site? Where
did they come from? How did they live? What did they believe
in? A whole new area of interest will be opened up to them and
here is an immediate justification for all those months of work.
Beyond it lie those deeper motivations for archaeology which
were discussed in the first chapter. Man needs a tangible past,
and archaeology provides it.

Suggestions for further reading

Two books which will take the reader a stage farther in his understanding of what the archaeologist is trying to do and how he approaches the task are *Archaeology and Society* by Grahame Clark and *Approach to Archaeology* by Stuart Piggott. Both discuss in greater detail the methods and techniques of archaeology, the problems of interpretation and the various methods of dating archaeological discoveries.

For those who prefer to turn next to the early history of archaeology itself, two highly readable books by Glyn Daniel may be recommended: *The Idea of Prehistory* and *The Origins and Growth of Archaeology*. General outlines of Old World prehistory are Stuart Piggott's *Ancient Europe* and Derek Roe's *Prehistory*.

All these have bibliographies which will lead the reader to more detailed studies and books on specialised topics.

Index

TEACH YOURSELF BOOKS

EXPLORING OUR INDUSTRIAL PAST
Kenneth Hudson

EXPLORING OUR INDUSTRIAL PAST could be described as industrial archaeology with people. It has been written in the belief that the history of industry and technology is as much about men and women as about factories, steam engines and spinning jennies, and that the point and fascination of studying the survivals of our industrial past is to discover more about the working skills and lives of our ancestors.

Kenneth Hudson has been writing, broadcasting and lecturing about industrial history for more than twenty years. Here he has written what is both a stimulating and a practical guide to the methods and techniques available to anyone for building up an understanding of how previous generations went about their work, their attitudes to it and how it in turn shaped their lives. These include the art of obtaining information from old people; the usefulness of museums; visiting old industrial buildings; and the importance of yesterday's catalogues and magazines.

There is also advice on writing up and publishing one's discoveries and on joining or forming societies, while an important section is devoted to the politics and realities of preserving industrial antiquities.

Front cover photographs taken at the Ultramarine ("Dolly Blue") works of Reckitt's (Colours) Ltd., Backbarrow, Cumbria.

Leisure, Domestic and General

ISBN 0 340 05960 5

TEACH YOURSELF BOOKS

ANALYTICAL PSYCHOLOGY

David Cox

There is no doubt of the immense value to be gained
from an understanding of Jung, but it is a formidable
task to begin a study of analytical psychology from
his original works. The aim of this book is to make his
ideas accessible at an introductory level and to
establish the essential concepts of Jungian
psychology.

The many conflicting views on psychology can
often appear confusing to the student. This book
meets this problem by outlining other contemporary
theories before going on to discuss the principal
concepts of Jungian psychology. But the central
theme is the same as that which ran through Jung's
life and work, a concern for the spiritual nature of
man and his need for self-knowledge.

Leisure, Domestic and General

ISBN 0 340 17886 8

UNITED KINGDOM   95p
AUSTRALIA $3.05 *
NEW ZEALAND $3.05
CANADA $3.75
*recommended but not obligatory

TEACH YOURSELF BOOKS

UNDERSTANDING SOCIAL ANTHROPOLOGY
David Pocock

This book argues that the vocation of social anthropology is to make the strange normal and the exotic familiar – that mankind is not represented solely or better by any one particular culture and that man can only understand himself by understanding all that he is and has been in a diversity of cultures throughout the world. Thus to look at other cultures as only strange and separate is to inhibit our capacity to understand ourselves as social beings.

The purpose of this book therefore is to stimulate an anthropological consciousness in the reader as a social being. A variety of cultures are presented in such a way that the reader can compare his or her own culture for the hidden similarities and significant differences, and exercises of an unusual kind are urged upon the reader to encourage this ability to think anthropologically.

At the centre of Professor Pocock's book is the idea that each one of us has a personal anthropology – assumed notions about such social values as kinship, authority, status and money. By becoming conscious of these notions through perceiving them anthropologically we can newly assess them and ourselves.

Leisure, Domestic and General

ISBN 0 340 20376 5

UNITED KINGDOM	£1.25
AUSTRALIA	$3.95*
NEW ZEALAND	$3.95
CANADA	$4.95

*recommended but not obligatory

TEACH YOURSELF BOOKS

SOCIOLOGY
J. H. Abraham

This book has been written to provide both the
student and the general reader with a basic but
comprehensive account of the principles and
practice of sociology. Beginning with an historical
narrative of the science from Plato to Comte and the
modern theorists, the book goes on to outline the
scope and methods of sociology. The author then
discusses the basic sociological concepts such as
social stratification, the family, the state, and social
control and mobility, and examines their significance
and interrelationship.

A clear, vivid and frequently personal picture of
both the development and the contemporary role of
sociology, particularly useful for those approaching
the subject for the first time, which does not avoid
the problems inevitably raised by any investigation of
social institutions. Now in a newly revised and
extended edition.

UNITED KINGDOM	75p
AUSTRALIA	$2.15*
NEW ZEALAND	$2.15
CANADA	$2.95

*recommended but not obligatory

ISBN 0 340 19819 2

TEACH YOURSELF BOOKS

PRINCIPLES AND PRACTICE IN MODERN ARCHAEOLOGY

David Browne

This book is based on the belief that there is a certain body of data that is traditionally the concern of the archaeologist and that this can only be discovered and studied by archaeological means — and that therefore archaeology is as much a subject in its own right as history.

The book begins by establishing the framework within which archaeologists work, the concepts on which their activity is based, before going on to examine the ideas and methods current in modern archaeology. The techniques of finding and excavating an archaeological site are described and separate chapters are devoted to the methodology of conservation of finds, on and off the site, and to the analysis of both organic and inorganic remains. The emphasis throughout is on the constantly advancing techniques of modern archaeology and on the necessity of developing expertise and professionalism in the field.

Anyone involved in archaeology, whether as a student or as an assistant at a 'dig', will find this book both relevant and informative. Above all it presents the major techniques of modern archaeology in such a way that can only increase archaeologists' understanding and enjoyment of their subject.

Leisure, Domestic and General

ISBN 0 340 19816 8

UNITED KINGDOM	£1.50
AUSTRALIA	$4.35*
NEW ZEALAND	$4.35
CANADA	$5.95

*recommended but not obligatory

TEACH YOURSELF BOOKS

HISTORY OF PHILOSOPHY
J. Lewis

In providing a historical narrative of philosophy, this book sets out to describe the chief rival attitudes towards life and its meaning, as they have developed during the history of Western thought.

To cover the history of philosophy from the Pre-Socratics through to Hegel, Whitehead and Popper is an immense task; in this slim volume Mr. Lewis has only attempted to communicate some insight into these philosophers' major ideas and their historical inter-action or conflict with each other.

As such, *History of Philosophy* will be read both by the reader who seeks to understand the development of thought in the West and by the student looking for an introduction to the major philosophers and philosophical movements of Western history.

Front cover: detail of *The School of Athens* by Raphael showing the philosophers Plato and Aristotle.

	UNITED KINGDOM	50p
	AUSTRALIA	$1.50*
	NEW ZEALAND	$1.45
ISBN 0 340 05617 7	CANADA	$1.95
	*recommended but not obligatory	